ONE IDEA
TO RULE THEM ALL

Reverse Engineering American Propaganda

MICHELLE STILES

ISBN: 979-8-9872946-0-4 (print)

Book Design: Lorie DeWorken, MindtheMargins.com
Cover image courtesy of Adobe Stock
Interior graphics in diagrams courtesy of Freepik.com

Printed in the United States of America

DEDICATION

To Alex, Chris,
Sofia and Bryce

For Freedom

"You cannot defeat a threat you choose not to define."

CONTENTS

INTRODUCTION

What if there are identifiable shortcuts that your brain utilizes to create settled beliefs, and what if those shortcuts have been "hacked" to influence you in ways you can't perceive?

Historically, this technique was called "manufacturing of consent," "crystallizing public opinion," "public relations," or just plain old "propaganda."

In today's world, these concepts are almost entirely ignored in high school and throughout academia in general. Most of your family and friends know little to nothing about them, and yet ignorance of them has devastating consequences for both individuals and society as a whole.

I'd like to rename the concept of propaganda as "Idea Bullying." Imagine the general discourse in the life of a nation as a swirling marketplace of ideas. We've been led to believe that the best ideas inevitably rise to the top. After all, isn't this why we have K-12 schools, colleges, universities, legislative debates, elections and town hall meetings?

But what if the game has been conned? What if the concept of civil debate has been thrown overboard—seemingly without our knowledge?

Idea Bullying is the ability to elevate favored ideas and

If we understand the mechanism and motives of the group mind, is it not possible to control and regiment the masses according to our will without their knowing about it?

EDWARD BERNAYS, *PROPAGANDA*

secure their adoption by the public through hidden and often nefarious means. The concept reflects the rude and sometimes violent nature of this underground insurrection.

Technically, debate still exists; talk shows and news prograing are found everywhere, but its core has been hollowed out. Democracy still exists, but its essence has been gutted, for one cannot survive without the other. The mechanisms created by the "Idea Bullies" drive most conversation—frequently in a subtle and devastating way.

The collection of tools needed to accomplish this coup was created in the early twentieth century from a small and inauspicious beginning to what has become a systemic juggernaut. One of the tools is called "Operation Sheepskin," which is the ability to amplify certain ideas and steer public opinion down a predetermined path toward specific ends that have been disguised as being in the public's best interest. Just like a megaphone is able to amplify sound for greater reach, the news media industrial complex is able to amplify and syndicate ideas throughout its vast networks. This power can be used to formulate and solidify story narratives in the mind of the populace before other explanations or alternative theories have the slightest chance to gain any traction or receive proper consideration.

"Operation Spider's Web" is a tool derived from Operation Sheepskin that is designed to reinforce and magnify Operation Sheepskin's power exponentially by creating a pseudo-reality which indeed is the very capstone of cultural deception.

The Idea Bullies surround you with Operation Sheepskin; working through apparently disconnected sources without your knowledge until, over time, you eventually receive the ideas spun by Operation Sheepskin as your very own.

These tools are capable of overwhelming three of the five core columns making up the natural infrastructure of belief: Authority (What Experts Think), Experience (Seeing

Is Believing), and Social Pressure (What Others Think and Do). The final two columns, Imagination (Cultural Stories) and Language (Framing the Debate), are highly susceptible to manipulation as well but are less targeted weapons.

The infrastructure of belief is the framework that aids decision-making; allowing us to make decisions safely without spending days and nights searching for raw data and facts.

This framework is stronger and more convincing than an army of facts. After reading this book, you will understand how and why "just the facts" fails to convince people time and time again—to the understandable frustration of millions.

As I sit here writing, the brouhaha over "fake news" rages on, with both sides of the political aisle vehemently pointing fingers at one another. But "What is fake news in reality?" and "Exactly who is promoting it?"

I hope to answer those questions without being expressly political. We are increasingly two hardened sides shouting each other down while a mystified, disgusted, and often apathetic middle group throws their hands up in frustration—certain there is no real truth to be had. This, too, is an end product of Operation Sheepskin.

The most effective way to destroy people is to deny and obliterate their own understanding of their history.
George Orwell

Just as with freezing water on a lake, so it is with Operation Sheepskin/Operation Spider's Web. At a critical tipping point, the ice becomes firm and impenetrable, trapping everything in a watery prison just below the surface.

Operation Sheepskin/Operation Spider's Web was created for just that sort of total planetary lockdown, and we are quickly moving to the critical moment of impenetrability.

It might seem like a nightmarish but far-off futurist novel if it were not so real and threatening.

So let's get started digging through the archives of history for the origins of the Idea Bullies and how they created Operation Sheepskin/Operation Spider's Web.

The endgame is to foster "pattern recognition" by closely

examining each aspect of Operation Sheepskin/Operation Spider's Web so that you can learn how to detect the velvety smooth Idea Bully, veiled in his many disguises, drowning out the competition and positioning "One idea to rule them all" to an unwary public—eager and willing to embrace it.

"One idea to rule them all,
One idea to find them,
One idea to bring them all.
And in the darkness bind them."

Chapter 1

SELLING A WAR?

Asked to name the first propaganda experts in the fledgling era of mass media and most people will respond with either the Germans or perhaps the Russians. But, in fact, it was the British and the Americans that first led the way. Surprised?

That's because we've been taught that propaganda involves telling people lies and falsehoods. In America, it is commonly thought that leaders generally tell the truth. The idea of outright propaganda seems far-fetched and exaggerated. And besides, we'd be wise to that in a heartbeat, right?

George Creel, head of the Committee on Public Information (CPI) during World War I, boasted after the war that the committee's efforts were a "vast enterprise in salesmanship, the world's greatest adventure in advertising."[1]

If "selling a war" sounds like a dubious proposition, you are probably in the majority. Shouldn't leaders have good reasons

1. George Creel, *How We Advertised America; the First Telling of the Amazing Story of the Committee on Public Information That Carried the Gospel of Americanism to Every Corner of the Globe* (New York, 1920), 4.

It was the fight for the minds of men, for the 'conquest of their convictions,' and the battle-line ran through every home in the country.
GEORGE CREEL,
HOW WE ADVERTISED AMERICA

either for or against entering a war?

The need to "sell" a war is highly questionable unless those being "sold to" have serious doubts and apprehensions, or those doing the selling lack solid and reasonable arguments.

As Creel famously put it, "Could we be sure that a hundred million—the fathers, the mothers, the children of America, alien born and native alike—understood well enough so that they would support one loan after another, would bear the burdens of taxation and send wave after wave of America's young manhood to die in Flanders fields?"[2]

Indeed, Americans were sold the idea that their precious sacrifices were necessary in order to "Make the world safe for democracy," a high-sounding yet rather nebulous goal that would remain elusive, ill-defined, and out of reach for years to come.

Boatloads of money and thousands of man-hours of volunteer labor were enlisted by the federal government across multiple forms of media in the United States and throughout the world—in short, a full-blown marketing campaign—to ensure success.

GEORGE CREEL AND THE COMMITTEE ON PUBLIC INFORMATION

Prior to the war, Creel was a progressive journalist who was heavily involved in Woodrow Wilson's reelection campaign. He was named to head the Committee on Public Information (CPI) on April 14, 1917, just six days after the United States had formally declared war on Germany.

History buffs may recall that Woodrow Wilson was re-elected for a second term on the platform slogan, "He kept us out of war." What most people don't know was that Wilson's

2. Ibid, 99.

odds of beating Charles Evans Hughes, a sitting supreme court justice and hugely popular former New York State governor, were stacked against him. When the campaign dust had cleared, Wilson had achieved the improbable on the strength of his powerful and novel campaign strategy.

Robert Wooley, a long-time journalist, ran his publicity bureau along the lines of a metropolitan daily, pumping out prepared material to be syndicated to more than a thousand newspapers. Teddy Roosevelt praised Wooley and his trusted ally George Creel by calling the victory the most brilliant achievement in the history of American politics.

When it seemed likely that the United States was going to enter the war, it was Wooley that urged President Wilson to form an expansive publicity bureau similar to his presidential campaign to sell the war effort.

President Wilson created the Committee on Public Information by executive order to consist of the Secretary of State, the Secretary of War, the Secretary of the Navy, and a civilian charged with the executive direction of the committee. In the absence of congressional hearings, laws, or administrative rules, the committee could be anything the President wished. Creel was quickly named by President Wilson to head the committee. Creel wasted no time in structuring it to serve as a clearinghouse of information concerning government activities and mobilizing artists, intellectuals, journalists, and other media professionals from around the country to utilize their skills on behalf of the war effort.

Arthur Bullard, a former student of Woodrow Wilson, was the first to advocate and publicly endorse the bureau. In *Mobilizing America*, Bullard spelled out his rationale for such a massive undertaking. The middle classes and the common man felt that this was a "businessman's war." Revolt and resistance were on the horizon unless this broad sentiment could be overcome.

World War I was the most colossal, murderous, mismanaged butchery that has ever taken place on earth. Any writer who said otherwise lied, So the writers either wrote propaganda, shut up, or fought.
ERNEST HEMINGWAY

Indeed, Britain was having trouble mobilizing the lower classes to fight, and Bullard envisioned similar problems in the United States unless action was taken to organize propaganda campaigns to make the struggle comprehensible—*and popular*.

In an alarming development for the western allies, the "little people" who were needed to fight the war were not toeing the line with enthusiastic support. After weeks of disappointing voluntary enlistments following the declaration of war, the United States Congress approved conscription with the Selective Service Act of May 1917. To deter draft evasion, local newspapers published lists of those who failed to register, and some "slackers" were even rounded up by volunteers from the American Protective League and jailed. Ultimately 24 million American men registered for the draft, and approximately 4.3 million were mobilized.

IN ORDER TO BRING DEMOCRACY ABROAD, MUST WE SUBMIT TO TYRANTS AT HOME.

The poem, *Red Feast*, penned by Ralph Chaplin, a leader of the Industrial Workers of the World (IWW), taunted those who would go and fight by calling them "fools." He mocked them for sacrificing their lives to the "Lords of War," wealthy capitalists living in ease who would profit handsomely from the gruesome purge.

Red Feast

Tear up the earth with strife
And give unto a war that is not yours;
Serve unto death the men you served in life
So that their wide dominions may not yield.
Stand by the flag—the lie that still allures;
Lay down your lives for land you do not own,
And spill each other's guts upon the field;
Your gory tithe of mangled flesh and bone.
But whether in the fray to fall or kill
You must not pause to question why nor where.
You see the tiny crosses on that hill?
It took all those to make a millionaire.[3]

Walter Lippmann, a newspaperman who will be examined later in more detail, was instrumental in laying out the specifics of the plan for the bureau at the request of President Woodrow Wilson. These plans were delivered to him on April 12th, two days before Creel was named and the executive order signed.

His ground plan included rallying a wide range of communication specialists to support the war effort, including people working in the motion picture industry. He also advocated intelligence functions for the bureau that would monitor foreign press and track down rumors and lies that would undermine American morale.[4]

---

3. Stuart Ewen, *PR! A Social History of Spin* (New York, 1996), 105-106.
4. Ibid, 108.

PROPAGANDA POSTERS, FILMS AND MORE

Creel built a broad, sweeping propaganda apparatus with the help of advertising agencies "that, in **scope and conception, transcended anything that had previously existed . . .**"in order to achieve the ideological mobilization of an entire nation and to sell America's vision of the war globally. This meant that an extensive fabric of persuasion would have to be knit.[5]

"How could the national emergency be met without national unity?" Creel inquired rhetorically. "The printed word, the spoken word, motion pictures, the telegraph, the wireless, the poster, the sign-board—all these were used in our campaign to make our own people and all other peoples understand the causes that compelled America to take arms."[6] Creel left no stone unturned to drive home the justness of America's cause.

The goal of the CPI was to impregnate the entire social fabric with the message of the war.

The extensive propaganda apparatus that Creel euphemistically titled "The House of Truth" included the following:

Division of News: News distributed statewide included press releases channeled through the mail and telegraph wires 24 hours/day; syndicated human interest feature pieces for magazines and publication of its own "Official Bulletin" targeting public officials, other newspapers, and any agency that distributed information.

Foreign News Division: News distributed internationally to offices in over thirty countries.

Advertising Division: Hundreds of advertisements and billboards were created, and thousands of dollars of free advertising space was solicited from newspapers for CPI use.

There was no part of the Great War machinery that we did not touch, no medium of appeal that we did not employ. The printed word, the spoken word, the motion picture, the telegraph, the cable, the wireless, the poster, the sign-board—all these were used in our campaign to make our own people and all other people understand the causes that compelled America to take arms.
GEORGE CREEL,
HOW WE ADVERTISED AMERICA

5. Ibid, 111.
6. Creel, 5.

Division of Pictorial Publicity: Volunteer artists, painters, sculptors, designers, illustrators, and cartoonists were recruited for the cause.

Division of Films: A "scenario" department, which drafted story outlines, was given to film producers for feature film production and distribution. The end products were *Pershing's Crusaders*, *America's Answer*, and *Under Four Flags*.

Academics: Well-known and respected academics were recruited to write "authoritative" pamphlets to justify the war effort.

Division of Speaking:

Four Minute Men: The support of local leaders, businessmen, or professional men were enlisted, to give what appeared to be extemporaneous speeches in local communities with whom they had influence. They were given detailed guidelines and sample speeches that included specific information and ideas to be conveyed. A typical speech might be given at the picture show in between the changing of the movie reels (see sample below).

Junior Four Minute Men: Enlisted the support of the best and brightest school-age youth by holding speaking competitions for elementary and secondary schools.

Speaking Circuit: The contact information for 10,000 speakers and 300 "super" speakers, who were both native- and foreign-born notables, were on file for large and small engagements.

National School Service Bulletin: Teachers were provided with topics and talking points for regular classroom discussion.

The "House of Truth" was designed and created to ensure that everyone was pulling in the same direction. For those who would not, censorship of dissenting ideas was monitored and codified as illegal.

Creel established the following acts and groups to suppress dissent:

Snitch Patrol: Four Minute Men were encouraged to identify, interrogate and even report people in their communities who expressed anti-war sentiment. When local shaming was not enough, laws were enacted.

The number of people advocating for peace reached its peak prior to the government crackdown of 1917–18. Ultimately, censorship was successful in stifling opposition to the war effort.

Espionage Act (1917): Upheld censorship of ideas considered deleterious to the war effort.

Sedition Act (1918): Made any criticism of the Wilson Administration illegal.

SAMPLE OF FOUR MINUTE MAN SPEECH

The following passage is a sample of a Four Minute Man speech, prepared by government speechwriters and given between reel changes at theaters by a local person who held authority in the community. The speech, which was made to look like a spontaneous expression of concern, was merely the rendition of government talking points.

While we sit here tonight, enjoying a picture show, are you aware that thousands and thousands of people in Europe—people not unlike ourselves—are languishing in slavery under Prussian masters? If we are not vigilant, their fate could be ours.

Part and parcel of the committee's success in mobilizing America's intellectual and curative resources for war was the simultaneous establishment of an ambience of censorship, calculated to discourage or punish impure thought.
STUART EWEN,
PR! A SOCIAL HISTORY OF SPIN

Now, then, do you folks here in Portland want to take the slightest chance of meeting Prussianism here in America? If not, then you'll have to participate in summoning all the resources of this country for the giant struggle. In addition to buying Thrift Stamps, and War-Savings Stamps to support our boys overseas, we must also hold fast the lines here at home.

To do this, we must remain alert. We must listen carefully to the questions that our neighbors are asking, and we must ask ourselves whether these questions could be subverting the security of our young men in uniform. You have heard the questions:

Is this, a Capitalists' war?

Was America deliberately pushed into the war by our captains of industry, for moneymaking purposes?

Are the rich coining blood into gold while the poor are taking on the greater burden?

Take heed. These questions are not innocent. They cannot be ignored.

These are questions constantly whispered by German sympathizers, openly asked by many others who simply do not understand. Our response to these questions is plain.

Our democratic system of income tax insures that the rates paid by those who are most well-off are greater than those rates paid by Americans who are less well-off. Tell those who ask such questions, that all Americans are sacrificing to defeat Prussianism, to make the world safe for democracy.

When you hear such questions, take heed. Do not wait until you catch someone putting a bomb under a factory. Report the man who spreads pessimistic stories, or who asks misleading questions, or who belittles our efforts to win the war. Send the names of such persons—even if they are in uniform—to the Department of Justice in Washington. Give all the details you can, with names of witnesses if possible.

Show the Hun that we can beat him at his own game. For those of you who are concerned for your own, or your family's safety, I can assure you that the fact that you made a report will never become public. Make the world safe for democracy! Hold fast the lines at home! [7]

IMAGINE WHAT THEY CAN DO NOW?

If you are more than a little bit surprised at the magnitude of effort, organization, and rhetoric used to "sell" the First World War, you are not alone. The CPI marketing campaign for World War I was the most expensive and most comprehensive campaign the world had ever known.

And, it was wildly successful!

Even though the Committee on Public Information was disbanded soon after the war, political and corporate leaders had seen a shining vision of a new era.

Public attitudes could now be manufactured with almost as much precision as physical items on an assembly line. Sure, there was still much more to learn, but there was no longer any need for slow and tedious methods of persuasion like reason and discourse.

The masses are never militaristic until their minds are poisoned by propaganda.
ALBERT EINSTEIN

7. Ewen, 102-103.

The race to refine and profit from the new mass persuasion techniques kicked into high gear and, in its wake, a profound shift in the landscape of civic life emerged. The republic would be hobbled going forward.

Barely one generation had passed since two men stood on a dusty stage in Illinois and debated the topic of slavery for nearly three hours on a hot August afternoon in 1858 with thousands in attendance listening to their every word. By means of telegraph and the railroad, news of the senatorial candidates, Abraham Lincoln and Stephen Douglas attracted national attention and spurred debate across the land. One debate wasn't enough . . . they held six more with the same brutal format consisting of a one-hour opening statement by the first candidate, a rebuttal lasting one and one half hours and a final thirty-minute rebuttal by the first speaker.

There was no more need for debate now that something easier and much more effective was at hand.

Unbeknownst to the populace, the shining light of a once great republic was being snuffed out.

Creation's highest achievement and the crowning glory of man, his reason and the quest for truth, outsourced to strangers and exchanged for a new reality; man as consumer—one who is sold "truth" by opinion shapers instead of striving and demanding to obtain them by reason. Subtle like a spring rain, the fall from grace took barely fifty years and dealt a devastating blow to republican governance without a single shot fired.

Chapter 2

ORIGINS OF MASS PERSUASION

Where on earth did Bullard, Creel, and Lippmann get their inspiration for the highly successful marketing of World War I?

Credit goes to Gustave Le Bon, a Frenchman who, in 1886, wrote *The Crowd: A Study of the Popular Mind*. It was a phenomenal success. According to Stuart Ewan, a Hunter College professor, Le Bon's book was translated into nineteen languages within a year and soon gained a wide readership among western elites such as Benito Mussolini, Adolf Hitler, Edward Bernays, Theodore Roosevelt, and Charles Dawes.

Le Bon declared the coming age, the "Era of Crowds" and was the first man to discuss the characteristics of a crowd and effective techniques for swaying the opinions of the multitudes without resorting to reason.[8] His book would ignite a revolution in governance.

At that time, it was popular to discuss the threats to order

Propaganda is to a democracy what the bludgeon is to a totalitarian state.
NOAM CHOMSKY, *MEDIA CONTROL: THE SPECTACULAR ACHIEVEMENTS OF PROPAGANDA*

8. Gustave Le Bon, *The Crowd: A Popular Study of The Mind* (New York, 1896, 2002), x.

that the crowd of "unwashed masses" presented to the ruling class. The shift from an agricultural to an industrial economy, the dislocation of the masses into cities, and the grievances arising from difficult working conditions led to the turmoil of numerous violent political revolutions, including the French (1789–99) and another series of revolutions on that shocked the European continent from 1820 through 1848. At the end of the 18th century, Le Bon suggested the elite were anxious and "uneasy with the threatening aspirations of the crowd and the destructions and upheavals foreboded thereby."[9] After all, the elites were few in number, and there were multitudes of the unwashed masses.

Le Bon opined that crowds were "like the sphinx of ancient fable: it is necessary to arrive at a solution of the problems offered by their psychology or to resign ourselves to being devoured by them."[10] In other words, eat or be eaten.

In the spirit of that attitude, Le Bon offered up ways for the crowd to be managed and tamed. His work instantly became a classic, embraced by leaders on both sides of the Atlantic.

BY ALL MEANS . . . DON'T APPEAL TO LOGIC

Le Bon's ideas undermined a fundamental tenet central to western thought: to change a man's opinion, you must appeal to his reason. The notion of man as a seeker of truth or any appeal to truth was fundamentally undercut. Ideas no longer needed to be explained, argued, or debated rationally in the era of crowds.

> The orators who know how to make an impression upon them always appeal in consequence to their sentiments and never to their reason. The laws of logic have no action on crowds.

9. Le Bon, 48.
10. Ibid, 61.

To bring home conviction to crowds, it is necessary first of all to thoroughly comprehend the sentiments by which they are animated, to pretend to share these sentiments, then to endeavor to modify them by calling up, by means of rudimentary associations, certain eminently suggestive notions, to be capable if need be, of going back to the point of view from which a start was made, and, above all, to divine from instant to instant the sentiments to which one's discourse is giving birth.[11]

According to Le Bon, the subconscious mind of the crowd could be manipulated, and the crowds held at bay through scientific means if one could learn the "tricks" of manipulating opinion.

This is the playbook the elites worldwide had been studying leading up to World War I. The marketing effort to sell the war was the demonstration project.

CROWD MANAGEMENT

The concepts Le Bon explored may seem simple to those who have grown up in the era of mass media, but they were truly revolutionary for their time.

Here is a small sample of wisdom from Le Bon's playbook.

Images, Words

The power of words is bound up with the images they evoke and is quite independent of their real significance. Words whose sense is the most ill-defined sometimes possess the most influence.

11. Ibid, 69–70.

Such, for example, are the terms democracy, socialism, equality, liberty, etc., whose meanings are so vague that bulky volumes do not suffice to precisely define it. Yet it is certain that a truly magical power is attached to those short syllables, as if they contained the solutions of all problems.[12]

Words that evoke powerful and sweeping images of connection, value, community, and fairness will be more effective than simple descriptive terms.

Ideas Simplified

Ideas, being only accessible to crowds after having assumed a very simple shape, must often undergo the most thoroughgoing transformations to become popular.

It is especially when we are dealing with somewhat lofty philosophic or scientific ideas that we see how far-reaching are the modification they require in order to lower them to the level of the intelligence of the crowds.

These modifications are dependent on the nature of the crowds, or of the race to which the crowds belong, but their tendency is always belittling and in the direction of simplification.[13]

One hundred years later, to present even a moderately complex idea during a debate would be considered anathema. In announcing the "Era of the Crowd, " Le Bon certainly foresaw the age of mass media and 30-second soundbites. Complex ideas must be jettisoned overboard like bad booze.

12. Ibid, 61
13. Ibid, 31.

The absurd reductionism of all ideas to the least common denominator is required for broad acceptance in the population.

Illusions

"Whoever can supply them with illusions is easily their master; whoever attempts to destroy their illusions is always their victim."[14]

A good example of this is politicians refusing to dispel the illusion that out-of-control spending by the government and trillions in debt is of no fiscal consequence. Destroying the illusion and making plans to cut services or raise taxes is always unpopular. It is easier and much more profitable for one's political career to kick the can down the road and let the masses have their illusion.

Experience

Experience constitutes almost the only effective process by which a truth may be solidly established in the mind of the masses, and illusion grown too dangerous be destroyed.

To this end, however, it is necessary that the experience should take place on a very large scale, and be very frequently repeated. The experiences undergone by one generation are useless, as a rule for the generation that follows, which is the reason why historical facts, cited with a view to demonstration, serve no purpose.[15]

Experience can be personal, as in having immediate knowledge of something (like being a victim of crime or police brutality, for example) or experienced vicariously through

14. Ibid, 67.
15. Ibid, 67–68.

the media.

It is a lived event for the current generation and holds more power than historical events. Think about the impact of the events of 9/11. If you were alive during that event, you remember exactly where you were and when you heard the news. It had and still has a powerful psychological force.

Affirmation

Affirmation pure and simple, kept free of all reasoning, and all proof, is one of the surest means of making an idea enter the mind of crowds. The more concise the affirmation is, the more destitute of every appearance of proof and demonstration, the more weight it carries.[16]

In other words, just declare it so, without any proof, and continue to do so regularly. Act as though others who question the affirmation are insane or deluded.

Repetition

Affirmation however has no real influence unless it be constantly repeated, and so far as possible in the same terms . . . The thing affirmed comes by repetition to fix itself in the mind in such a way that it is accepted in the end as a demonstrated truth.[17]

Repetition across the different elements of Operation Spider's Web is even more effective than throughout the news media complex itself, as we shall see later in Chapter 8.

16. Ibid, 77.
17. Ibid, 77.

Contagion

When an affirmation has been sufficiently repeated and there is unanimity in this repetition . . . what is called a current of opinion is formed and the powerful mechanism of contagion intervenes. Ideas, sentiments, emotions, and beliefs possess in crowds a contagious power as intense as that of microbes.[18]

This power is a consequence of the social reality that most people do not want to be singled out for going against the grain. Once an idea has reached a critical threshold of adoption, dissenters will have an uphill battle to sway the tide or even maintain opposing viewpoints.

Imitation

Men, like animals, have a natural tendency to imitation. Imitation is a necessity for him, provided always that the imitation is quite easy. It is this necessity that makes the influence of what is called fashion so powerful. Whether in the matter of opinion, ideas, literary manifestations, or merely of dress, how many persons are bold enough to run counter to the fashion?[19]

The worldwide Operation Sheepskin/Operation Spider's Web makes this tendency even more formidable.

Prestige/Authority

Prestige/Authority in reality is a sort of domination exercised on our mind by an individual, a work, or an idea.

18. Ibid, 78.
19. Ibid, 79.

This domination entirely paralyses our critical faculty, and fills our soul with astonishment and respect . . . Prestige is the mainspring of all authority. Neither gods, kings, nor women have ever reigned without it.[20]

Authority goes hand in hand with status in society. For many, the medical establishment and science hold places of unquestioned authority and influence. For some, the church or the Pope is their main authority. For others, celebrities, successful businessman and/or sports figures are the most influential.

I've expanded Le Bon's categories slightly and explained the older, less well-understood term "prestige" below:

Acquired Prestige/Authority: Authority that results from name, fortune and reputation. Acquired prestige is based on titles like being a doctor or a lawyer, family name and reputation, and/or being highly successful.

Personal Prestige/Authority: Authority that is associated with a characteristic peculiar to the individual. It may co-exist with reputation, glory, and fortune or be strengthened by them.

Personal prestige is based on being a highly charismatic person or having desirable character qualities that draw and attract others to their influence.

Manufacturing Ideas

The success of World War I showcased to many astute observers the power of using Le Bon's methods in the age of mass media.

20. Ibid, 81.

Propaganda had always existed, of course, but was vastly limited to one man speaking to a small crowd. By using Greek fallacies and shrewd rhetoric, crowds could be tricked and manipulated to sway opinions.

What was new was both the techniques Le Bon had inspired as well as the incredible reach of the "new" media tools that could be used to broadcast and disseminate the message well beyond one nation to the far reaches of the world. Techniques like affirmation, repetition, and contagion fit hand in glove with mass media as a force multiplier.

In reality, only the massive financial resources of a country made it possible to instill a singular message through diverse mediums for such an extended length of time.

One man's reach had morphed into a surround sound of media broadcasting the same message through different channels, thus magnifying the effect on any one individual.

One man's speech could be readily discounted, but the repetition from apparently divergent sources was powerful and difficult for the average man to resist alone.

All in all, the campaign was a spectacular success in mobilizing a nation toward the goal of full and unwavering support for a war that many felt was a sham.

Men like Edward Bernays and Walter Lippmann took notice of the unleashed powers and rushed to put them into practice.

Bernays, a foot soldier in World War I, became the father of public relations and seeded Le Bon's method into major corporations like Philip Morris, Dodge, Chiquita, and Proctor and Gamble.

Lippmann took his jaded opinion of the unthinking populace with him into journalism, where he rose to prominence and critical acclaim in the news world despite the bitter irony of his instrumentality in fostering the demise of journalism.

A sinister idea took shape; if public attitudes could be so easily shaped and molded, even in the face of significant

The tantalizing thought that the leaders of society could actually manufacture ideas and inject them into the population in such a manner as to win wide reaching assent without the slow and tedious need for reason and discourse was proven correct.
—ADOLF HITLER

resistance and in light of the enormous sacrifices on the line for the populace, was there anything that could not be "sold" in like manner?

What further need was there for appeals to reason and debate to influence society?

Ideas could be manufactured at will.

Chapter 3

TOO STUPID FOR DEMOCRACY?

The prevailing opinion of the news media is that it serves as an independent source committed to discovering and reporting the truth.

Our founding fathers enshrined freedom of the press into the First Amendment of our Constitution for a reason. A free press separates democracies from dictatorships by giving reporters who represent the people both the power and the duty to hold the powerful accountable by bringing truth to the masses.

Journalists do not simply report events as powerful people wish to have them reported. Or do they?

Noam Chomsky, an American linguist and philosopher, hypothesized this exact scenario in *Manufacturing of Consent* (1988).

Leaders of the media claim that their news choices rest on unbiased professional and objective criteria, and they have support for this contention in the intellectual community.

> *If, however, the powerful are able to fix the premises of dis-*
> *course, to decide what the general populace is allowed to see,*
> *hear, and think about, and to "manage" public opinion by*
> *regular propaganda campaigns, the standard view of how*
> *the system works is at serious odds with reality."* [21]

As we learned from the first two chapters, one of the suc-
cesses of World War I was the changing of attitudes toward
democracy and the news.

> *The propaganda efforts of the CPI reinforced a growing belief*
> *that ordinary men and women were incapable of rational*
> *thought. For democracy to work effectively, public opinion*
> *needed to be guided by what historian Robert Westbrook has*
> *characterized as "enlightened and responsible elites."* [22]

A growing post-war consensus was unveiled among the
intelligentsia that perceptions needed to be managed for the
people. Ironically, Walter Lippmann (1889–1974), heralded as
the "most influential journalist of the 20th century," the "Father of modern journalism," and winner of two Pulitzer Prizes,
emerged as an avid proponent for the radical restructuring of
journalism's role in society.

For more than forty years, he exerted unprecedented influence on public opinion in America through his syndicated
newspaper column "Today and Tomorrow." Popularly understood, he was a journalist of the first rank.

Unbeknownst to most of his popular readership, Lippmann wrote books disparaging the public at large and critical
of their ability to function as intelligent members of society,
marginalizing democracy as a "failed" project.

*No serious sociologist
any longer believes that
the voice of the people
expresses any divine or
specially wise and lofty
idea. The voice of the
people expresses the mind
of the people, and that
mind is made up for it by
the group leaders in whom
it believes and by those
persons who understand
the manipulation of
public opinion. It is
composed of inherited
prejudices and symbols
and clichés and verbal
formulas supplied to them
by the leaders.*

—Edward L. Bernays,
Propaganda

21. Noam Chomsky, *Manufacturing Consent,* (New York, 1988), x.
22. Edward Bernays, *Crystallizing Public Opinion,* 18.

To those who knew him or examined his writings, his anti-democratic leanings easily emerged. To a friend, he stated, "The size of the electorate, the impossibility of educating it sufficiently, the fierce ignorance of these millions of semi-literate, priest-ridden, parson-ridden people have gotten me to the point where I want to confine the actions of majorities." [23]

MEDIA SELECTION DISTORTION

Lippmann's propaganda work during World War I "made him realize how easily public opinion could be manipulated, and how often reporters and editors distorted the news." [24]

For example, it was possible to magnify German casualties by the constant repetition of certain formulaic phrases such as 'the enemy exhausted by his losses has not renewed the attack' and 'according to prisoners, the German losses in the course of the attack have been considerable,' without regard to the actual realities on the battlefield, thereby creating the illusion that the Germans were being beaten badly and that the allies were winning.

Lippmann remarked that "We have learned to call this 'propaganda.' A group of men, who can prevent access to the event, arrange the news of it to suit their purpose." [25]

Lippmann explained that by putting dead Germans in the focus of the picture, and by omitting mention of the French dead, a very specific view of the battle was created. In other words, visual arrangement of images could benefit one version of reality over another.

He goes on to say,

---

23. Steel, Ronald, *Walter Lippmann and The American Century*, (Boston, 1980), 217.
24. Ibid, p. 172.
25. Walter Lippmann, *Public Opinion*, (Virginia, 1922, 2010), 26.

Without some form of censorship, propaganda in the strict sense of the word is impossible. In order to conduct propaganda, there must be some barrier between the public and the event. Access to the real environment must be limited, before anyone can create a pseudo-environment that he thinks wise or desirable.[26]

The media are less a window on reality, than a stage on which officials and journalists perform self-scripted, self-serving fictions.

—THOMAS SOWELL,
THE VISION OF THE ANOINTED: SELF-CONGRATULATION AS A BASIS FOR SOCIAL POLICY

Foreign events, as well as battlefield events or any other events where public access is restricted, can be easily manipulated. Distance from an event and restricted access to events make the public more reliant on others for information, and confirmation of actual events is often difficult or next to impossible to obtain.

Trusting that journalists are trying to present the truth and not just a predetermined version of it is an essential component of the journalists' relationship to the people.

PICTURES OF A PSEUDO ENVIRONMENT

According to Lippmann, men hold pictures or images of the complex modern world around them, acting as shortcuts to understanding and functioning as springboards to action. These pictures are simplifications of the world in a story format. For example, the Marxist conceives of the world as revolving around class consciousness and acts accordingly. National consciousness is another way of conceiving the world. A man situated within a broader story relies on it to give structure to his day-to-day decisions.

The way the world is imagined determines at any particular moment what men will do . . . But what is propaganda, if not the effort to alter the picture to which men respond?[27]

26. Ibid, 27.
27. Ibid, 19.

Lippmann argued that an audience must participate in the news, much as it participates in a drama, by personal identification. The press could provide a reader with familiar footholds from which he can enter a story. For example, calling an association of plumbers a "combine" sanctions a feeling of hostility and, conversely, calling those same plumbers "a group of leading businessmen" sanctions a favorable reaction.

Reporters and editors were sitting in commanding seats of power, creating the pictures from which Americans formed their view of the world. The news media could completely distort the way an event was perceived through what parts of the original story they chose to omit and what they chose to retain. After all, there is only so much time in a thirty-minute newscast or only so many words allotted in any newspaper column to describe an event.

The meaning of intricate, perplexing, and often veiled modern events could be condensed and summed up with simple pictures having narratives that an organized intelligence wished to portray.

Indeed, Lippmann advocated for just that sort of inversion of the typical news workflow. The narrative or points of emphasis for any particular event are selected by experts and fed to newsroom editors, who then select images and headlines to represent and support that storyline to ensure that the public perceives the event in the desired fashion, accuracy and truth be damned.

Public opinions must be organized for the press if they are to be sound, not by the press as is the case today.[28]

This is what Lippmann meant by a pseudo-environment. Without insight into the actual event, Americans would be

28. Ibid, 22.

none the wiser about what was being done . . . night after night.

REPRESENTATIVE GOVERNMENT WILL NOT WORK

Lippmann, in *Public Opinion* (1922), argued that the modern world had become so complex and the issues so distant from the common man that it was impossible for the masses to have an accurate opinion on most public issues.

He argued that with neither the time nor the inclination to research the facts, the average citizen was encumbered by local biases and prejudices that made him a poor prospect to render fair and impartial conclusions affecting the future of the nation.

Lippmann's conclusion was that representative government was bound to fail unless the citizenry could rely on experts who would interpret and organize complex data for the masses and steer them to the best decisions.[29]

Lippmann, however, continuously confused democracy with representative government. In a representative government, the people need not be supremely informed on every topic. Rather representatives, chosen through elections, are entrusted to dig up the facts and make choices on their constituents' behalf.

WHO ORGANIZES THE OPINIONS?

Instead of trusting the representative process, Lippmann believed that a technocracy of sorts should evaluate the options at hand, make decisions and then organize the story for the media.

The real sequence should be one where the disinterested expert first finds and formulates the facts for the man of

In regard to propaganda the early advocates of universal literacy and a free press envisaged only two possibilities: the propaganda might be true, or the propaganda might be false. They did not foresee what in fact has happened, above all in our Western capitalist democracies — the development of a vast mass communications industry, concerned in the main neither with the true nor the false, but with the unreal, the more or less totally irrelevant.
—ALDOUS HUXLEY,
BRAVE NEW WORLD REVISITED

---

29. Ibid.

action, and later makes what wisdom he can out of comparison between the decisions, which he understands and the facts, which he organized.[30]

Who are the so-called disinterested experts Lippmann was talking about? Are they politicians, scientists, academics or perhaps some other group?

If experts are put in charge of the press, who is left to speak truth to power and hold the government agencies and politicians accountable? Who would hold disinterested experts accountable? Is it possible to find truly disinterested experts to wield that kind of power in a selfless manner?

Ultimately, the acclaimed newsman Lippmann thought very little of the people reading his daily opinion pieces and advocated the transformation, if not the outright destruction of the very foundation of news itself, a quest for the truth and holding the powerful accountable.

Lippmann's insidious views, born out of the rumble of World War I, essentially sanctioned the infiltration of news media with deception under the guise of bettering society. As one can see from the following, Lippmann's advocacy was a stark departure from the ideal of the press as conceived by the founding fathers of our first colonies.

A list of early variations of Constitutions or Bill of Rights in the Thirteen Colonies that enshrined freedom of the press as essential:

1. **A Declaration of the Rights of the Inhabitants of the Commonwealth of Massachusetts. – June 15, 1780:** *XVI. The liberty of the press is essential to the security of freedom in a state: it ought not, therefore, to be restrained in this Commonwealth.*

30. Ibid, 201.

2. **A Declaration of the Rights of the Inhabitants of the Commonwealth or State of Pennsylvania – September 28, 1776:** *XII. That the people have a right to freedom of speech, and of writing, and publishing their sentiments; therefore the freedom of the press ought not to be restrained.*

3. **A Declaration of Rights, and the Constitution and Form of Government agreed to by the Delegates of Maryland, in Free and Full Convention Assembled. – November 11, 1776:** *XXXVIII. That the liberty of the press ought to be inviolably preserved.*

4. **Virginia Declaration of Rights – June 12, 1776:** *XII That the freedom of the press is one of the greatest bulwarks of liberty and can never be restrained but by despotic governments.*

5. **North Carolina, A Declaration of Rights, &c. – December 18, 1776:** *XV. That the freedom of the press is one of the great bulwarks of liberty, and therefore ought never to be restrained.*

6. **An Act for Establishing the Constitution of the State of South Carolina. – March 19, 1778:** *XLIII. That the liberty of the press be inviolably preserved.*

7. **Constitution of Georgia; February 5, 1777:** *ART. LXI. Freedom of the press and trial by jury to remain inviolate forever.*

8. **A Declaration of the Rights of the Inhabitants of the State of Vermont – July 8, 1777:** *XIV. That the people have a right to freedom of speech, and of writing and publishing their sentiments; therefore, the freedom of the press ought not be restrained.* (Vermont was not a state yet but saw fit to set up a Declaration of Rights.)[31]

31. https://www.colonialwilliamsburg.org/learn/living-history/freedom-press-eyes-founding-fathers.

Upton Sinclair: Lippman's Contemporary

In 1919, Upton Sinclair published a brutally honest insider's view of the sordid and unethical behavior of the press over the course of his lifetime as a muckraking investigative journalist. Best known for his expose on the meat packing industry, "The Jungle," Sinclair's personal knowledge of powerful corporate interests exerting leverage to manipulate public opinion and thwart reform contrasted vividly with Lippmann's lofty and naive appeal for some benevolent and selfless organized intelligence to take charge of the press. Sinclair lamented that he exposed owners and editors not as individuals but as a social force, not because they lied about him, "but because a new age of fraternity is trying to be born, and they, who ought to be assisting the birth [the press], are strangling the child in the womb."[32]

In story upon story, Sinclair catalogs the corrupting forces of owner self-interest, the influence of advertising dollars, direct bribes, the ability to slander and defame opponents of a political or social position and the ownership and control of the Associated Press, a news bureau syndicating stories across the country thus magnifying their impact, by a small number of voting shareholders, i.e., the media owners.

Rise of Consolidation

Since Lippmann's time, ownership of media in the United States has been consolidated over and over until a small number of privately owned corporations control most of the media real estate.

While appearing as independent entities discreet from the government and committed to holding politicians accountable, are they really?

32. Sinclair, Upton, *The Brass Check: A Study Of American Journalism; Evidence and Reasons Behind The Media's Corruption*, (France, 1919), viii.

In 1963, there were 1,500 different owners of television and radio stations. Twenty years later, in 1983, only 50 companies comprised 90% of the media; by 2011, that number had dwindled to a mere 6 companies. Those companies and some of their main holdings are listed below.

General Electric (Comcast, NBC, Universal Pictures, Focus Features)

News Corp. (Fox, Wall Street Journal, New York Post)

Disney (ABC, ESPN, Pixar, Miramax, Marvel Studios)

Viacom (MTV, Nick, JE, BET, CMT, Paramount Pictures)

Time Warner (CNN, HBO, Time, Warner Brothers)

CBS (Showtime, Smithsonian, NFL.com, Jeopardy, 60 Minutes)

To make matters worse, a Sonoma State University research project investigated the overlap of media boards of directors (a total of 118) with boards of top international corporate companies and found that they occupied seats on another 288 corporate boards. For instance, one particular New York Times board member also sat on the boards of the Carlyle Group, Eli Lily, Ford, Johnson and Johnson, and Hallmark.

A *Washington Post* board member was included on the boards of Lockheed Martin, Coca-Cola, Dun & Bradstreet, and Gillette. It stands to reason that corporate interests play a large role in media bias. Is it really possible for the *Washington Post* to critique defense contract overruns by Lockheed Martin or for the *New York Times* to be objective in handling stories about drug recalls?

Could corporations be acting in collusion with politicians for their own benefit? Could they be advancing narratives of their own for increased profit margins? Or is there some other group of "experts" behind both corporations and politicians controlling narratives? These are important questions as we continue to explore the history of Idea Bullies.

CIA INFILTRATION

In 1975, the Church committee uncovered what was called "Operation Mockingbird," a clandestine CIA project to infiltrate the news media with narratives that favored CIA interests written by actual CIA assets or journalists on the take.

The CIA began a systematic infiltration of the corporate media in the late 1940s—a process that often included uncomfortably close relationships between the CIA and leaders of major outlets like CBS. William Paley, founder of CBS and a wartime colonel, was a firm believer in "all forms of propaganda." In order to foster loyalty to the Pentagon, Paley hired CIA agents to work undercover at the behest of his close friend, Allen Dulles.

This close collusion between the media and the CIA was highlighted in a 2017 documentary by John Barbour entitled *The American Media & The 2nd Assassination of President John. F. Kennedy*.

The movie effectively exposes what can only be described as a coordinated media effort to establish the narrative of a lone gunman, peddle the credibility of the Warren Commission's sham investigation, and sabotage the viability of New Orleans district attorney Jim Garrison's legal case that tied the CIA to the assassination of President Kennedy.

Barbour exposes example after example of the American media being shockingly partisan and wantonly disinterested in truth. The viewer can observe Dan Rather, a young, fresh-faced reporter from Dallas, explaining to his audience that he has just been allowed to see the Zapruder film, a home movie that captured the exact moment of Kennedy's assassination. Looking soberly into the camera, Rather emphasizes the forward movement of Kennedy's head, suggesting a gunshot from the rear, a critical point of emphasis in order to "validate" the lone gunman theory.

TIMELINE OF MEDIA WHISTLEBLOWERS

1908	*Career of a Journalist* by William Salisbury
1919	*Brass Check* by Upton Sinclair
1926	*My Own Story* by Fremont Older
1938	*Lords of the Press* by George Seldes
1938	Rise of Journalism as a Profession [First graduate School of Journalism at University of Missouri]
1942	"A Free and Responsible Press" [Report Created by The Commission on Freedom of the Press financed by Henry Luce of Time, Inc., a classic exercise in whitewashing the growing concern over media corruption]

RISE OF TELEVISION

1962	*The Image: A Guide to Pseudo-Events in America* by Daniel J. Boorstin

KENNEDY ASSASSINATION

	Strong censoring of any criticism of Oswald Narrative and media collusion [Mark Lane Books]
1975	The Church Committee [Exposed CIA assets in the News]
1977	*Rolling Stone Magazine* [Exposed Operation Mockingbird]
1979	*Roosevelt, Churchill, and the World War II Opposition* by George Eggleston
1985	*Amusing Ourselves to Death: Public Discourse in an Age of Show Business* by Neil Postman
1992	*JFK Assassination: The Jim Garrison Tapes* by John Barbour
2017	*The Smear: How Shady Political Operatives and Fake News Control What You See, What You Think and How You Vote* by Sharyl Attkisson
2019	*Presstitutes Embedded in the Pay of the CIA: A Confession from the Profession* by Udo Ulfkotte
2020	*Slanted: How the News Media Taught Us to Love Censorship and Hate Journalism* by Sharyl Attkisson

The problem is that to any honest observer, the Zapruder film, withheld from public scrutiny for nearly ten years, clearly shows Kennedy's head moving violently backward as a bullet enters his right forehead. Rather, an obscure talent at the time went on to an illustrious media career despite being guilty of one of the most glaring factual inaccuracies of the 20th century.

This documentary clearly illuminates the media's role in quickly establishing the storyline and discrediting all competing narratives that compete for attention and validation. If you were still under any illusion that the Media is only interested in establishing the truth, this is a must-watch.

Media Decline

In view of the incredibly long historical record of media corruption, why is it so hard to see propaganda masquerading as news in a democracy? How is it possible that the dark black secrets of the media can be called out again and again, and yet trust has remained until relatively recently?

In the past, isolated voices of criticism could be silenced. A few well-placed lies to damage the reputation of the critic would do wonders to deflect accusations of corruption, as Upton Sinclair readily attested. Attacks on a person's reputation were not easily undone, spreading across the public domain like wind-swept dandelion seeds despite the occasional perfunctory retraction at a later date. How was it possible for ordinary citizens to fight back? The average citizens didn't have near enough money to take on the media giants.

Or the cartel could simply ignore its critics. Other than book publishing, there were few means to counter such a powerful and expansive network. This power differed by orders of magnitude compared to the impact of a single book. Looking back through history, the lone voices of whistleblowers can be found.

In countries where the levers of power are in the hands of a state's bureaucracy, the monopolistic control over the media, often supplemented by official censorship, makes it clear that the media serve the ends of a dominant elite. It is much more difficult to see a propaganda system at work where the media are private and formal censorship is absent.
Noam Chomsky,
Manufacturing of Consent

Recently, however, a crack in the armor of the media cartel has been exposed. A growing segment of the population feels the mainstream media can no longer be trusted to provide the truth and is seen instead as promoting agendas benefiting unseen forces, and this is reflected in falling advertising revenues and dwindling readership, adversely affecting the financial standing of some of the world's most "respected" publications.

More and more people are asking why news stories seem biased and agenda-driven. And if any average Joe Citizen with a cell phone and a social media account can broadcast details of an event that the media is leaving out and, even worse, contradict accepted media narratives, what is actually going on? The answer lies with control.

Too many people now have access to an event and are able to read the tea leaves for themselves based on the record of numerous witnesses. Try as they might, the media cartel is losing its monopoly on news, despite the efforts to control the Internet and social media. But wait, here comes a "crisis" that they can fix.

FAKE "NEWS" CRISIS

The current "fake news" crisis is mostly a diversion from the "real news" crisis and systemic media corruption that has been metastasizing for over one hundred years—and this is something that few are talking about. It is the seed of Lippmann's ideology coming to fruition.

People on the Left think that FOX news is peddling "fake news," while people on the Right think CNN and MSNBC are trafficking in "fake news." Both are wrong.

Images are conjured up of news outlets brazenly disseminating outright false or misleading stories.

In reality, what constitutes false and misleading reporting need only be subtle shifts in emphasis—a rather fine line of

THE MAKING OF NEWS
A Sacred Trust

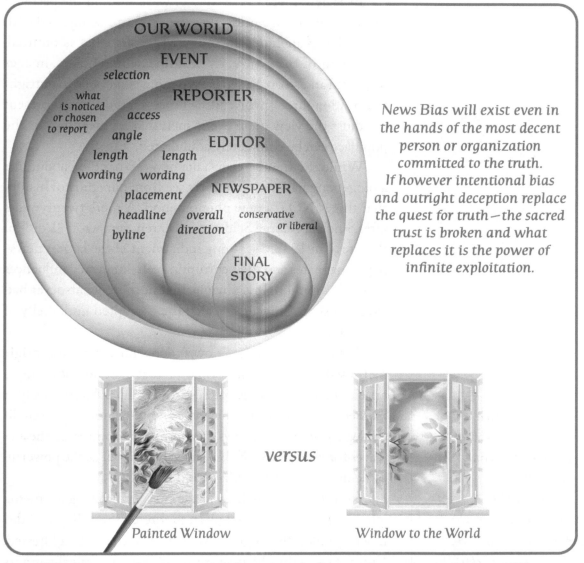

OUR WORLD

EVENT

selection

what is noticed or chosen to report

REPORTER

access

angle

length

wording

placement

headline

byline

EDITOR

length

wording

NEWSPAPER

overall direction

conservative or liberal

FINAL STORY

News Bias will exist even in the hands of the most decent person or organization committed to the truth. If however intentional bias and outright deception replace the quest for truth—the sacred trust is broken and what replaces it is the power of infinite exploitation.

Painted Window

versus

Window to the World

"The power to determine each day what shall seem important and what will be neglected is a power unlike any that has been exercised since the Pope lost his hold on the secular mind." —WALTER LIPPMAN distorting the truth as opposed to outright lies, such as was demonstrated earlier in the chapter and that has been ongoing since the early nineteen hundreds.

In review, there is a myriad of ways, even in the best and most honorable of worlds, that the news can be injected with bias; what is included in the news versus what is omitted, placement of the article, its headline, word choices, images displayed and so on. Video is even more vulnerable to outright falsification through the editing process if the intent is present to adjust the view of an event such that its meaning for the populace can be completely adulterated.

While the trendy term "fake news" is bandied about like a ping-pong ball, we can clearly see from our study of history that this is NOT a new phenomenon. A mere twenty years after Sinclair, George Seldes, a career reporter, wrote "Lords of the Press" in 1938, a scathing indictment of the largest newspaper magnates and their corrupting self-interested influences on public opinion. It is obvious that nothing whatsoever had changed since Sinclair revealed the corrupted underbelly of the news.

The term "fake news," now a global buzzword, was originally used to refer to disinformation that masquerades as news articles or videos and is often spread online. Alternatively, it has been co-opted by politicians, especially Trump, to discredit the legacy or network news media that has dominated the airwaves for years, ABC, NBC, and CBS, as well as the powerful cable networks such as CNN and MSNBC.

As a result, journalists, academics, and the legacy media joined efforts in a fevered pitch to foretell the collapse of democracy unless the "urgent problem" of fake news be addressed. Enter stage right, the magical solution that ironically grants the legacy media and big tech giants like Facebook, Google, and Twitter god-like powers to render judgments about what constitutes truth in society.

If people in the media cannot decide whether they are in the business of reporting news or manufacturing propaganda, it is all the more important that the public understand that difference, and choose their news sources accordingly.
—THOMAS SOWELL

Seizing the moral high ground, they have exploited the situation and are now heavily invested in sanitizing the news and social media platforms to prevent "misinformation" in the form of verification checkmarks, fact-checkers and "authenticated news."

In reality, what is being accomplished is the purge of alternative viewpoints that challenge the legacy media narrative—a new cloak for the old tactic of censorship. Seen from a historical perspective, the fox lobbying (corrupted media) to be in charge of the hen house (what is or is not *real* news) can now be identified for what it is—mere subterfuge.

We can see in this scenario the "problem, reaction, solution" formula, which will be discussed later in the book, being harnessed by Big Media to create an even greater monopoly over "news."

Lippmann stated frankly that news and truth were not the same thing. "The function of news is to signalize an event . . . and make a picture of reality upon which men can act." [33]

According to Lippmann, the troubles of representative government can all be traced to this one common source . . . "the people who are compelled to act without a reliable picture of the world, who have violent prejudices, are apathetic, prefer the curious trivial over the mundane important and hunger for sideshows and three-legged calves." [34]

Flying in the face of a mountain of historical evidence suggesting that it would be folly to outsource truth to experts via the news and media, yet that is exactly what Lippmann recommends.

In conclusion, kudos to Lippmann for saying the quiet part out loud . . . you ARE too stupid for democracy, and from now on, we WILL be organizing the story to suit a hidden agenda . . . for your benefit, of course.

33. Lippmann, *Public Opinion*, 194.
34. Ibid, 197.

In the next chapter, we'll explore how to "manufacture" news itself.

After all, why wait for an event to unfold when you can create one and tailor the narrative to fit your need.

Chapter 4
THE INGENIOUS TECHNIQUE OF STAGECRAFT

In light of the success achieved by propaganda during the war effort, many were eager to hop on the public opinion-shaping train—including corporations, academics and politicians. Why not utilize this new science in the service of corporate profits? After all, ad space was expensive and often ineffective. Could it not also be used in peacetime in the service of general or electoral politics?

A young Edward Bernays knew the answer.

As a young man during World War I, Bernays served with the Committee on Public Information and quickly recognized that "what could be done for a nation at war could be done for organizations and people in a nation at peace."[35]

One of the first to see the potential of what had been unleashed during the war and harness its power, Bernays recognized that public opinion could now be influenced almost

---

35. Scott M. Cutlip, *Public Relations, The Unseen Power: A History*, (New Jersey, 1994), 168.

at will. With this knowledge in hand, he began to work side by side with the corporate community, eager to test this new and exciting way to manipulate the public mind.

Harkening back to Le Bon, who foretold of experience as one of the most "effective processes by which a truth may be solidly established in the mind of the masses and illusions grown too dangerous be destroyed,"[36] Bernays elevated the technique of using staged experiences, passed off as news, to an art form.

Through this technique, it was possible to reach the public in a way that would blind them to the fact that they were being sold a bill of goods.

Coverage by the news media signaled to the masses that an idea or issue was important. It also galvanized "newsworthy" experiences to broad national audiences, magnifying their influence many times above what could be accomplished by local dissemination alone and much more authentically than possible through direct advertising.

It's a shameful moment for U.S. media when it insists on being subservient to the grotesque propaganda agencies of a violent, aggressive state.
—Noam Chomsky

THE INVENTOR OF STAGECRAFT

By 1928, the year he published the book *Propaganda*, Bernays (considered the founder of modern public relations) was already in a class by himself and the staged event his trademark deception. Simply handing out a press release took little intelligence. The true craft was in discerning what news "looked and tasted like" so that "news" could be easily created for a client, something that would stand out while not appearing to be staged.

> *The public relations counsel must lift startling facts from his whole subject and present them as news. He must isolate ideas and develop them into events so that they can be more readily understood and so they can claim attention as news.*[37]

36. Le Bon, 67.
37. Bernays, 22–23.

Many years later, Bernays called it the science of "creating circumstances." To this day, public relations experts hold to similar but more advanced stagecraft techniques.

MARKETING PIANOS

Bernays was soon applying this method to everything under the sun, including piano marketing. Imagine if Bernays could transform the task of selling a piano from a "hard sell" to creating a popular demand that made purchasing a piano a necessity to complete a trendy and culturally astute music room.

The transformation from "hard sell" to meeting a "demand" that has been ingeniously and unwittingly sown into the minds of people is a decisive transformation. *Keep this in mind as we move along.*

In the meantime, consider how Bernays weaves his magic in the marketing world. Remember, the magic doesn't just belong to sales.

If, for instance, I want to sell pianos, it is not sufficient to blanket the country with a direct appeal, such as:

"YOU buy a Mozart Piano now. It is cheap. The best artists use it. It will last for years."

The claims may all be true, but they are in direct conflict with the claims of other piano manufacturers, and in indirect competition with the claims of a radio or a motorcar, each competing for the consumer's dollar.

What are the true reasons the purchaser is planning to spend his money on a new car instead of on a new piano? Because he has decided that he wants the commodity called "locomotion" more than he wants the commodity called music? Not altogether. He buys a car, because it is at the moment the group custom to buy cars.

The modern propagandist therefore sets to work to create circumstances, which will modify that custom. He appeals perhaps to the home instinct, which is fundamental. He will endeavor to develop public acceptance of the idea of a music room in the home. This he may do, for example, by **organizing an exhibition** *of period music rooms designed by well-known decorators who themselves exert an influence on the buying groups. He enhances the effectiveness and prestige of these rooms by putting in them* **rare and valuable tapestries.**

Then, in order to create dramatic interest in the exhibit, he **stages an event or ceremony.** *To this ceremony* **key people,** *persons known to influence the buying habits of the public, such as a famous violinist, a popular artist, and a society leader,* **are invited**. *These key people affect other groups, lifting the idea of the music room to a place in the public consciousness it did not have before.*

The juxtaposition of these leaders, and the idea which they are dramatizing, are then **projected to the wider public through various publicity channels.** *Meanwhile,* **influential architects have been persuaded** *to make the music room an integral architectural part of their plans with perhaps a specially charming niche in one corner for the piano. Less influential architects will as a matter of course imitate what is done by them whom they consider master of their profession. They in turn will implant the idea of the music room in the mind of the general public.*

The music room will be accepted because it has been made the thing. And the man or woman who has a music room, or has arranged a corner of the parlor as a musical corner, will naturally think of buying a piano. It will come to him as his own idea.

Under the old salesmanship the manufacturer said to the prospective purchaser, "Please buy a piano." The new salesmanship has reversed the process and caused the prospective purchaser to say to the manufacturer," Please sell me a piano.[38]

Shockingly, the sophistication of these "sales" tactics is nearly one hundred years old, and yet how many remain blinded to their use? Later Bernays was retained by Phillip Morris and challenged with breaking down the social taboo that prevented respectable women from smoking.

What follows is the reprinted story of how Bernays deftly stitched together a campaign that was by all accounts a stunning financial success for his client and the entire tobacco industry. The manufactured circumstance helped hoodwink the public and shatter the cultural barrier that had protected women from the evils of smoking. Bernays transfigures the hard sell of a commodity into a desire for equality with men, an alchemy, and a dark art with immense ramifications.

TORCHES OF FREEDOM

The women hired for the project had to be convincing and appealing enough to influence the masses, yet not too good looking or "model-y" so as to give truth to the vamp stereotypes. Edward Bernays set about designing the Torches of

---

38. Bernays, *Propaganda*, 77–78.

Freedom campaign, a PR stunt the first of its kind in the world.

On 31st March 1929, at the height of Easter Parade, a young woman named Bertha Hunt stepped out into the crowded fifth avenue [sic] and created a scandal by lightning [sic] a Lucky Strike cigarette. The incident was highlighted even more because the press had been informed in advance of Hunt's course of actions, and had been provided with appropriate leaflets and pamphlets.

What they did not know was that Hunt was Bernays's secretary and that this was the first in a long line of events that was aimed at getting women to puff. Bernays proclaimed that smoking was a form of liberation for women, their chance to express their new found strength and freedom.

While walking down the street Hunt told the New York Times that she first got the idea for this course of action when a man on the street asked her to extinguish her cigarette as it embarrassed him. "I talked it over with my friends, and we decided it was high time something was done about the situation." The New York Times dated 1st April 1929 ran a story titled, "Group of Girls Puff at Cigarettes as a Gesture of 'Freedom.'" As women all over the country took to this newfound symbol of their emancipation aggressively, Bernays must have had the last laugh at the ironic date of the story.

Ten young women followed Bertha Hunt that day down Fifth Avenue, brandishing their torches of freedom. The audience's imagination was captured as newspapers enthusiastically reported on this new scandalous trend. Bernays used "sexual liberation as a form of control." The days that followed saw Bernays not only emphasizing the liberation movement for women as far as cigarettes were concerned, but also waxing eloquent on its slimming properties and glamour quotient that ensured women getting hooked to Lucky Strikes. Sales doubled from 1923 to 1929.[39]

When covered by the press, the importance of staged events like "Torches of Freedom" was falsely magnified. In fact, there was no woman or group of women who felt so passionately inspired by the idea of smoking that they were willing and motivated to organize this "protest." By faking the event and publicizing it, the public had the very vivid impression that significant numbers of women were clamoring to smoke and convinced that their equality with men entitled them to do so.

In 1928, Bernays frankly stated:

This practice of creating circumstances and of creating pictures in the minds of millions of persons is very common. Virtually no important undertaking is now carried on without it, whether the enterprise be building a cathedral, endowing a university, marketing a moving picture, floating a large bond issue, or electing a president.[40]

Politicians Share the Fun

But should corporations have all the fun using stagecraft? No, indeed. Bernays made sure that political leaders could benefit from using sophisticated event creation strategies as well. Bernays mockingly criticizes a politician as outdated and worn,

39. https://yourstory.com/2014/08/torches-of-freedom.
40. Bernays, *Propaganda*, 52.

who thinks that appealing to reason by using the radio to disseminate his argument will be successful. Even though he may be able to reach millions of listeners, it is a frontal head-on confrontation of ideas and should be avoided at all costs.

Bernays advocates instead a well-planned strategy that results in a coordinated campaign designed to dramatize the issue to the people before the candidate ever addresses the issue at hand. This way, he is seen to be responding to the people and the questions that the dramatization has stirred up.

For example, let's say that a politician supported low taxes on imports, things like wool that currently had high import taxes.

> *He would have groups, whose interests were especially affected by the high cost of living, institute an agitation for lower schedules. He would dramatize the issue; perhaps by having prominent men boycott woolen clothes, and go to important functions in cotton suits, until the wool schedule was reduced. He might get the opinion of social workers as to whether the high cost of wool endangers the health of the poor in winter.*[41]

In all these ways, a master strategist is seeding into the public consciousness the "evils "of high taxes on imported goods. At the right time, the politician merely steps forward to play on the strings of swirling interest. He advocates for low import taxes and rescues the people agitating for relief under heavy burdens. What a nice story, you say? Exactly. Our brains are wired for story.

Debate, reasoning, and the appeal to truth were now passé. Bernays showed how the savvy political leader could orchestrate events, dramatize issues, steer public opinion, and create demand for a predetermined solution waiting in the wings— just off stage.

41. Ibid, 121–122.

Dramatizations would be created to appear as organic grassroots concerns percolating in and through the population at large, creating the illusion of spontaneous synchronicity. Subsequent tailored "interventions" would be supplied later by astute political leaders. Only after the collective national mind had been primed in this manner, would a political leader take a stand to influence the national "discussion."

In reality, no discussion was intended—or desired. The staged sequence of events was choreographed to win support for the predetermined outcome regardless of the merits of the issue.

Modern Stagecraft

It is important to include one more modern example, so the reader does not think this is an archaic technique relegated to the dustbin of history.

A powerful example of modern stagecraft can be found in the Kuwait witness, an anonymous fifteen-year-old girl who testified before the Congressional Human Rights Caucus on October 10, 1990. She stated at the time that she had been a hospital volunteer and a firsthand witness to the terrifying act of Iraqi soldiers pulling premature infants from incubators and leaving them to die on the cold floor of the hospital. This story had been circulated by American news agencies again and again in the months that preceded the entry of the United States into the Persian Gulf War in the winter of 1991, attesting to the barbarism of the Iraqi military and causing moral outrage against the atrocities.

Her identity was supposedly kept secret at the hearing to ensure her safety following her testimony. Years later, it eventually came to light that the girl's name was Nayirah al-Sabah, daughter of the Kuwaiti ambassador to the United States and that she had witnessed no such atrocities being committed. So how was it that she was called to testify to the United States congress?

She had been recruited, as had all the witnesses that day, by Gary Hymel, vice president of Hill and Knowlton, one of the largest public relations firms in the world. His agency was on the payroll of the Kuwaiti royal family in exile and had been assigned the task of building support for the intervention of the United States in Kuwait.[42]

If you are stunned at the prospect of a Congressional committee having all their witnesses for an inquiry provided by a public relations firm, you are not alone. Is it possible that the committee members were blind to this "small" detail? Wouldn't there be some long entrenched system to ensure the authenticity of witnesses before Congress? The press could be taken to task as well for the failure to verify witnesses. Remember, this story had circulated in the press for some time BEFORE the committee hearing. How did the story initially get into the press, and how was it funneled broadly across diverse organizations and corporations without someone, anyone attempting to verify the authenticity of the event? Wouldn't the press want to interview multiple witnesses? Surely Hill and Knowlton could not have directly handed a press release to the New York Times on such an important topic and been taken seriously, or had they?

The false accusation and gross misrepresentation given sanction by the United States government not only went unchallenged but was disseminated far and wide and used as justification for its involvement in the conflict between Iraq and Kuwait.

As can be seen by these examples of stagecraft, the medium of the news was the vehicle for deception in all cases.

---

42. John R. MacArthur, T*he Second Front: Censorship and Propaganda in the Gulf War* (New York, 1992). 58–59.

A cooperative and compliant relationship with the news media—lapdog comes to mind—would be of paramount importance in facilitating ongoing deceptions to be perpetrated on the unsuspecting public.

As we saw in the last chapter, Lippmann led the way years earlier for this sort of manipulation to emerge by justifying the uncoupling of journalistic integrity with the search for truth. Later this unholy marriage between the agencies attempting to manufacture public consent, those that hired them and the news was further facilitated with the advent of Operation Mockingbird, which involved the infiltration of CIA assets into journalist positions across numerous media platforms in the 1940s.

Though most people don't know his name, Edward Bernays' influence on modern society is perhaps more far-reaching than that of his famous uncle, Sigmund Freud. Bernays, at the ripe age of 98, summed up the essence of the "public relations" (read "propaganda") expert.

> As a member of that intellectual elite who guides the destiny of society, the PR, "professional," Bernays explained, aims his craft at a general public that is essentially, and unreflectively, reactive. Working behind the scenes, out of public view, the public relations expert is "an applied scientist," educated to employ an understanding of sociology, psychology, social psychology, and economics to influence and direct public attitudes . . . A highly educated class of opinion-molding tacticians is continuously at work, analyzing the social terrain and adjusting the mental scenery from which the public mind, with its limited intellect, derives its opinion.[43]

43. Ewen, 10.

"Adjusting the mental scenery" is a type of shorthand for the ability to alter reality from which the public instinctively and reflexively shapes its opinions.

At the most basic level, staged events create pictures of reality that are not true. "Actors" surrounding the staged picture tell stories about the events, which are then interpreted as the official narrative.

If the staging were unmasked and the truth of the matters known, people would rightly feel that they had been duped and misled by the false interpretation. The practitioners of this craft cannot help but take a dim view of the subjects upon which they act.

STAGECRAFT: A RICH MAN'S SPORT

So let's be honest: In the game of manipulating the minds of men, not many have the resources to play the game effectively. A quick look back at the bolded text in the Piano Marketing example earlier in this chapter reveals the length and breadth of the extent to which Bernays went in order to change public opinion.

The objection to propaganda is not only its appeal to unreason, but still more the unfair advantage which it gives to the rich and powerful.
—BERTRAND RUSSELL, *SKEPTICAL ESSAYS*

Costs would be significant to stage an exhibition, obtain rare and valuable tapestries, put on a ceremony with the rich and/or famous, publicize those events, and finally persuade influential architects to modify their designs to favor a pet project. From this one example alone, it is obvious that stagecraft and propaganda is a costly endeavor.

Creel boasted that the expenditure of the Committee on Public Information only cost American taxpayers $6,850,000. The actual cost, after taking into account the financial contributions of thousands of volunteers who freely gave their time and talent to the war effort as a matter of patriotism, would be substantially greater.

Using an inflationary calculator, the cost of the campaign for WWI would be $145,576,672 in today's market (2018).

In 1929, Bernays was paid $25,000 ($364,021 accounting for inflation) by Lucky Strike to implement the Torches of Freedom campaign.

Cracking that market, as George Washington Hill (the owner of Lucky Strike) said, would be "like opening a new gold mine right in our front yard"—and indeed it was. Corporations that stood to make millions could afford Bernays's exorbitant charges.

PEOPLE OF THE WEST AND FREEDOM OF SPEECH

One of the foundational ideals of Western democracy is freedom of speech. Freedom of speech allows for the unfettered circulation of ideas to be sorted through by the young and old, the rich and poor, and lays the foundation for a veritable marketplace of ideas.

Richard Weaver, a long-time University of Chicago professor and cultural critic, argues that the tradition of the West based on individual freedom has never supported the right of a single voice or narrative to prevail exclusively. He argues that the evolutionary process of allowing each group to win support for its ideas is critical sausage-making to the eventual adoption of an idea and that "truth acquired in this manner is possessed more fully and securely than one which is adopted without having to meet the test of competition."[44]

Freedom of the press is guaranteed only to those who own one.
—A. J. LIEBLING

This is why the paid promotion of a single narrative is necessarily anathema to democratic ideals.

Long live the competition of ideas.

---

44. Ted Smith, ed., *In Defense of Tradition: Collected Shorter Writings of Richard Weaver, 1929–1963,* (Indiana, 2000), 307.

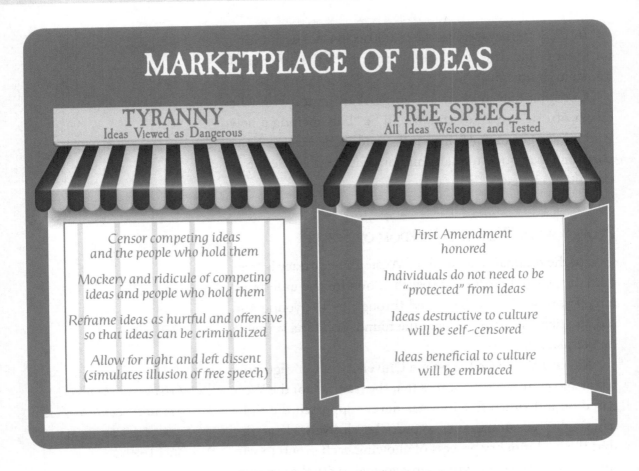

MARKETPLACE OF IDEAS

TYRANNY
Ideas Viewed as Dangerous

*Censor competing ideas
and the people who hold them*

*Mockery and ridicule of competing
ideas and people who hold them*

*Reframe ideas as hurtful and offensive
so that ideas can be criminalized*

*Allow for right and left dissent
(simulates illusion of free speech)*

FREE SPEECH
All Ideas Welcome and Tested

*First Amendment
honored*

*Individuals do not need to be
"protected" from ideas*

*Ideas destructive to culture
will be self-censored*

*Ideas beneficial to culture
will be embraced*

WHO WILL WIN THE WAR OF IDEAS?

If, as Weaver states, a true democratic society is a marketplace of ideas, it is important for all ideas to have a level playing field in order to be heard, discussed, accepted, or rejected—even bad ideas. Financial resources that enable someone to purchase an especially large megaphone for the purpose of expanding the reach of their ideas while drowning out or suppressing others' ideas will create a power differential in society.

Acknowledging the reality of this unequal playing field, Bernays dryly noted: that there was little chance that the millions of housewives who were concerned about the health effects of manufactured foods would have their concerns translated into real changes in society unless their demand could be organized, dramatized and made evident to the legislators who had the power to effect those changes through legal means. This meant propaganda, and this meant large sums of money.

But of course, most housewives or even a collection of housewives do not have the money needed to organize and sustain propaganda campaigns with their staggering expenses. Who will speak for them? The reality is that those who are able to control the mechanisms of propaganda, paid promotions, event creation, the purchase of spokespeople, etc., will be the undisputed winners in the war of ideas. Other very fine or even exceptional ideas risk being irrevocably lost.

Bernays lays out the naked ideology that underlies his callous message to the housewives: only select individuals with deep pockets can play the game at the top of the pyramid.

This reality is a cold, bracing slap in the face to people who dismiss the menace of propaganda by jocularly contending that it can be used for good or bad. While that may be true, only governments, large organizations and corporations have the means to play the propaganda game by utilizing all the potent weapons at their disposal through the media.

The Internet has been revolutionary in giving the "little guy" a voice once again in democracy; anyone with a computer, a blog or an iPhone can get his message out. But a lone voice is no match against coordinated campaigns that utilize all aspects of media by saturating the public with "one idea to rule them all."

In today's world, mammoth financial and technological resources are well positioned to outpace and overwhelm small voices of opposition.

If by chance and diligence small voices begin to gain traction in the public mind, Operation Sheepskin can be turned on and turned against individuals in order to castigate, demonize and belittle those ideas and the people who hold them.

Game over. Or is it?

I think the subject which will be of most importance politically is mass psychology . . . Its importance has been enormously increased by the growth of modern methods of propaganda. Of these the most influential is what is called 'education.' Religion plays a part, though a diminishing one; the press, the cinema, and the radio play an increasing part . . . It may be hoped that in time anybody will be able to persuade anybody of anything if he can catch the patient young and is provided by the State with money and equipment.
—BERTRAND RUSSELL

Chapter 5
UNDERGROUND MENACE

American propaganda: reality or oxymoron? This almost shocking juxtaposition of words jars our senses. What happened? How did this concept become so hidden? Tracking the word "propaganda" from intense interest to relative obscurity will help uncover the lost menace.

BACKLASH TO WAR TIME PROPAGANDA

Following World War I, the explosive power of using coordinated campaigns to influence the attitudes and opinions of an entire nation attracted the attention of devotees and critics alike. In 1935, Harold Lasswell, an assistant professor of political science at the University of Chicago, commented that "The practice of scientific propaganda has permeated the Great Society until scientists and laymen view it today with curiosity and even with alarm."[45]

45. Harold Lasswell, Ralph D. Casey, Bruce Lannes Smith, *Propaganda and Promotional Activities: An Annotated Bibliography*, (Illinois, 1935), ix.

I know of no country in which there is so little independence of mind and real freedom of discussion as in America ... In America the majority raises formidable barriers around the liberty of opinion; within these barriers an author may write what he pleases; but woe to him if he goes beyond them. Not that he is in danger of an auto-da-fe, but he is exposed to continued obloquy and persecution. His political career is closed forever, since he has offended the only authority (i.e., majority opinion) which is able to open it.
—ALEXIS DE TOCQUEVILLE, *DEMOCRACY IN AMERICA*

A small but significant number of people were radically awakened to the shocking menace of propaganda.

Bernays accurately pinpoints the real potential and the true danger in this new technique:

If we understand the mechanism and motives of the group mind, is it not possible to control and regiment the masses according to our will without their knowing about it? [46]

Rightly understood, the new propaganda was a radically different phenomenon that modern man was struggling to articulate and reconcile with twentieth-century life.

The unique potential that mass media now afforded the propagandist and the growing list of techniques available to successfully bypass reason were celebrated by some and of grave concern for others.

Debates and discussions ensued in academia, town halls and editorials across the land.

The Social Science Research Council Committee on Pressure Groups and Propaganda, formed in 1931, included distinguished scholars of the academic world, most notably represented by the field of political science. The intention of the committee was to stimulate scientific analysis of the function of propaganda and to investigate the existing state of research. To that end, they initiated a series of conferences that eventually led them to publish a detailed bibliography as a tool for future sophisticated research in the area.

The book consists of four hundred pages of bibliographies listed according to categories and by the council's own admission is limited; so great was the volume of material available.

Those looking to minimize concern over the potential dangers tried to redefine the word propaganda by stripping it

46. Bernays, *Propaganda*, 71.

of its powerful implication of menace. "Nothing to see here, folks—move along."

Proponents like Ivy Lee, a publicity agent and a contemporary of Bernays, declared "propaganda" a neutral technique that could be used for good or bad but which was, in and of itself, harmless. Citing the potential benefit of large-scale propaganda campaigns employed in the public interest, adherents downplayed the dangers and dismissed those who cautioned against the wholesale embrace of the new technologies as "alarmists."

However, rehabilitation of the word "propaganda" faced an uphill battle.

Despite notable men like Bernays, championing the word and its use in his book *Propaganda*, the general public's antipathy toward the word was too great to overcome. Publications such as Arthur Ponsonby's *Falsehood in War Time* and Philip Bibbs's *Now It Can Be Told* exposed the practices of the wartime propagandists and created a strong sentiment of outrage and anger within segments of the population at the mercy of those campaigns. A spirit of "never again" pervaded the land.[47]

Harold Lasswell, a University of Chicago professor and author of *Propaganda Technique in the World War* (1938), powerfully expressed the feeling of betrayal felt by the country in the aftermath of the great war such that even the word "propaganda" carried an ominous clang. Feelings of being duped, degraded, and vexed at the unknown cunning trick to which they had been subjected pervaded earnest souls.

That credulous utopianism, which fed upon the mighty words, which exploited the hopes of the mass in war, has in many minds given way to cynicism and disenchantment,

47. Smith, 303–304.

and with these earnest souls propaganda is a far more serious matter.

Some of those who trusted so much and hated so passionately have put their hands to the killing of man, they have mutilated others and perhaps been mutilated in return, they have encouraged others to draw the sword, and they have derided and besmirched those who refused to rage as they did.

Fooled by propaganda? If so, they writhe in the knowledge that they were blind pawns in the plans which they did not incubate, and which they neither devised, nor comprehended, nor approved.[48]

You perceive the force of a word. He who wants to persuade should put his trust not in the right argument, but in the right word. The power of sound has always been greater than the power of sense . . . Give me the right word and the right accent and I will move the world.

—JOSEPH CONRAD

As a result of this antipathy, Lasswell declared, "it was common for modern promoters of attitudes to borrow the prestige of words like education, information, public relations and publicity."[49]

While the word "propaganda" fell into disuse, the techniques or tools of the trade steadily advanced under different, more discrete terminology. Despite the term "propaganda" going underground, the study and use of it never abated.

The topic has been splintered and parsed into diverse fields of studies draped under the cover of the social sciences. Bernays, well advanced in years, opined to Stuart Ewen, Chair of the Department of Film and Media Studies at Hunter College, who wrote *PR! A Social History of Spin* reinforced that notion by stating that "The public relations expert was referred to as an applied scientist, educated to employ an understanding of sociology, psychology, social psychology, and economics to influence and direct public attitudes."[50]

48. Harold Lasswell, *Propaganda Technique In The World War*, (New York, 1938), 2–3.
49. Lasswell, *Propaganda And Promotional Activities*, 3.
50. Ewen, 10.

FORGOTTEN MENACE

In the decade following World War I, propaganda awareness was at its zenith, and the public was keenly aware of its dangers. However, this was to be short lived.

Even as propaganda practitioners in the United States were dissociating themselves from the term, its use skyrocketed once again around the advent of World War II. However, this time the term was applied repeatedly and exclusively in reference to enemy communications.

Oh, a blessed day for the propagandist! The true threat of propaganda to those living in the United States slipped into the forgotten past—leaving the true menace of this modern leviathan hidden behind a shroud of mist. In the public mind, an incontestable conclusion had been drawn: Democracies simply do not engage in propaganda. End of story.

Never has there been a more profound and miraculous metamorphosis of the definition of a word in all of history.

"Propaganda" was so thoroughly embedded into the concept of the enemy's behavior that the real threat—that it could and would be used in America—had vaporized into thin air.

Since those earlier days, Americans have remained extremely susceptible to manipulation through propaganda. Without the common usage of the word to remind us of its reality, tragically, we have forgotten the dangerous menace the Idea Bullies represent to our republic and how they severely jeopardize our ability to self-govern.

Robert Kirsch of the Los Angeles Times summed up the dangers of propaganda in a review of *Propaganda: The Formation of Men's Attitudes* by Jacque Ellul—one of the few deep reflections on propaganda since World War II: "Propaganda . . . is not only destructive to democracy, it is perhaps the most serious threat to humanity operating in the modern world."[51]

---

51. Robert Kirsch, "Los Angeles Times Review" (from back cover): Jacques Ellul. *Propaganda The Formation of Men's Attitudes*, (New York, 1965).

EDUCATION TO SAVE THE DAY?

In 1938, at the height of the post-WWI furor over propaganda, businessman and philanthropist Edward Filene joined hands with other leaders to create The Institute of Propaganda Analysis. This organization was dedicated to protecting democracy from the threat of propaganda.

While their efforts were laudable, the institute failed miserably in its quest to create an operational definition of "propaganda." Early attempts at definition pushed the narrative that deciphering motives was the only way to separate "good propaganda" from "bad propaganda." Bernays roundly mocked the newly formed institute by laughing at the suggestion that divining motive was possible in real life. Bernays was right—this method proved to be a dead end.

Not to be dissuaded, the Institute tried again to unlock the puzzle of propaganda detection, this time by having citizens ask the question, "Whose end does the propaganda serve?" or, in other words, "Who benefits or 'Cui bono?'" Just like the difficulty in determining who benefits in a murder mystery, the ability to draw these inferences in the analysis of propaganda might require a team of investigators. Sneaky propagandists are not so stupid as to telegraph their own self-interests, nor would they be in the near future.

The Institute turned instead to the task of arming citizens with the basics in critical thinking or at least an "easy-to-learn" version of the age-old Greek fallacies identified during the Greco-Roman era now modernized and re-packaged as the "Seven Propaganda Techniques."

Here are the seven techniques as laid out by the Institute:

1. **Name Calling:** A device to discredit an opponent without refuting his claim.

2. **Glittering Generalities:** A device that identifies a position with "virtue" by use of words like truth, freedom, democracy, liberty, etc.

3. **Transfer:** An appeal which seeks to carry over the authority, sanction, or prestige of something we respect and never to something else.

4. **Testimonial:** A device to use the opinion of an expert authority for propaganda purposes.

5. **Plain Folks:** An appeal to win confidence by appearing to be like the common people being addressed.

6. **Card-Stacking:** An appeal that uses under-emphasis or over-emphasis to dodge issues and evade facts.

7. **Band Wagon:** An appeal that encourages us to follow the crowd because "Everybody is doing it."

Clyde Miller, associate professor at Columbia Teachers' College and co-founder of the Institute, exemplified the growing incoherence of the movement with this statement about the importance of learning how to think in a democracy:

"They [the students] must learn how to think independently, and they must also learn how to think together . . . So far as individuals are concerned, the art of democracy is the art of thinking and discussing independently together."

Moving even further into the weeds, the Institute released the ABCs of Propaganda Analysis in its December 1937 edition, consisting of the following:

ASCERTAIN the conflict element in the propaganda you are analyzing. All propaganda contains a conflict element in some form or other—either as cause, or as effect, or as both cause and effect.

BEHOLD your own reaction to this conflict element. It is always necessary to know and to take into consideration our own opinions with regard to a conflict situation about which we feel strongly, on which we are prone to take sides. This information permits us to become more objective in our analysis. **[Conflating propaganda with prejudice.]**

CONCERN yourself you today's propagandas associated with today's conflicts. These are the ones that affect directly our income, businesses, working conditions, health, education and religious, political and social responsibilities. It is all too easy to analyze some old example of propaganda, now having little relation to vital issues. **[History is critical to understand the development of the art.]**

DOUBT that your opinions are "your very own." They usually aren't. Our opinions, even with respect to today's propagandas, have been largely determined for us by inheritance and environment. **[Conflating propaganda with prejudice or beliefs.]**

EVALUATE, therefore, with the greatest care, your own *propagandas*. We must learn clearly why we act and believe as we do with respect to various conflicts and issues—political, economic, social, and religious. **[Conflating propaganda with prejudice or beliefs.]**

FIND THE FACTS before you come to any conclusion. There is usually plenty of time to form a conclusion and believe in it later on. Once we learn how to recognize propaganda, we can most effectively deal with it by suspending our judgment until we have time to learn the facts and the logic or trickery involved in the propaganda in question. We must ask:

Who is this propagandist?

How is he trying to influence our thoughts and actions?

For what purpose does he use the common propaganda devices?

Do we like his purposes?

How does he use words and symbols?

What are the exact meanings of his words and symbols?

What does the propagandist try to make these words and symbols appear to mean?

What are the basic interests of this propagandist?

Do his interests coincide with the interests of most citizens of our society as we see it? **[Divining intentions is very different than determining "the facts."]**

GUARD always, finally, against omnibus words. They are the words that make us the easy dupes of propagandists. Omnibus or carryall words are words that are extraordinarily difficult to define. They carry all sorts of meanings to the various sorts of men. Therefore, the best test for the truth or falsity of propaganda lies in the specific and concrete definitions of the words and symbols used by the propagandist. Moreover, sharp definition is the best antidote against words and symbols that carry a high charge of emotion.[52]

While the last piece of advice seems reasonable, notice the dubious use of the word "propagandas" multiple times, conflating propaganda with prejudice or a belief structure. Instead of taking their own advice to properly define terms, they hopelessly distort and confuse. One almost gets the impression this is "propaganda" about "propaganda."

The magnitude of the Institute's failure can only be fully demonstrated if one fast-forwards to the feeble attempts of modern-day educators to tackle a problem now one hundred years in the making and vastly more sophisticated as compared to the nineteen thirties.

Renee Hobbs, Professor and director of Media Education at the University of Rhode Island and author of *Mind Over Media: Propaganda Education for a Digital Age*, has been studying propaganda for decades. She asserts that propaganda education, critical for democracy, is often missing entirely from school curriculums or is taught in outdated ways (read "outdated" as circa 1930s).

Imagine the National Council of Teachers of English was forced to issue a resolution in 2019 advocating students be allowed to learn how to analyze propaganda in a "post-truth" society instead of being restricted to deliberative dialogue only.[53]

52. Alfred McClung Lee & Elizabeth Bryant Lee, *e (1939). The Fine Art Of Propaganda; A Study of Father Coughlin's Speeches,. The Institute for Propaganda Analysis.* (Harcourt, Brace and Company, 1939), 16–18.
53. https://www.gse.harvard.edu/news/21/03/harvard-edcast-propaganda-education-digital-age.

Hobbs, who prefers the term Media Literacy, claims that propaganda is an essential part of the democratic process and that it is both the cause and cure for what ails us. Her materials are being broadly distributed in the schools and yet do little to clear up hopelessly muddied waters.

Ultimately, when the menace of propaganda is written out of the operational definition, the train has jumped tracks at the start and is destined for failure. One cannot defend against a threat that remains undefined. There are plenty of terms for "good" propaganda; persuasion, debate dialogue, even influence. Let's use them.

What began as the brainchild of a young Mr. Bernays has steadily grown into a multibillion-dollar social engineering industry utilizing highly sophisticated campaigns and long-term strategies for opinion shaping and even for creating alternative realities—as you will see in the coming chapters. Trying to shield citizens against such efforts by arming them with a few Greek fallacies or Media Literacy is like going into a knife fight with a lollipop.

Modern educators might think their approach is sufficient. However, you will begin to realize how narrow and inaccurate current thinking really is when contrasted with a comprehensive propaganda model. Sadly, these grossly inadequate teachings are still used in school systems across the country. No wonder we are sitting ducks for propaganda.

Ultimately, The Institute of Propaganda Analysis failed miserably to protect democracy because its members failed to capture and define the real craft and, therefore, the real menace. If they expected to be successful, they should have studied Le Bon so they could understand what I call the "Infrastructure of Belief."

To Le Bon, we must return, for he holds the key to understanding the true scope of propaganda and the targets of its action.

NEVER allow the enemy to define your terms. If you want to win a war of propaganda, you must be able to manipulate language to expose the truth.

—Jenifer Mohammed, *Resurrecting Cybele*

Propaganda works best when those who are being manipulated are confident they are acting on their own free will.

—Joseph Goebbels

thou shalt not commit logical fallacies

PLATO   SOCRATES   ARISTOTLE

strawman
Misrepresenting someone's argument to make it easier to attack.

false cause
Presuming that a real or perceived relationship between things means that one is the cause of the other.

the fallacy fallacy
Presuming that because a claim has been poorly argued, or a fallacy has been made, that it is necessarily wrong.

slippery slope
Asserting that if we allow A to happen, then Z will consequently happen too, therefore A should not happen.

ad hominem
Attacking your opponent's character or personal traits in an attempt to undermine their argument.

appeal to emotion
Manipulating an emotional response in place of a valid or compelling argument.

personal incredulity
Saying that because one finds something difficult to understand that it's therefore not true.

special pleading
Moving the goalposts to create exceptions when a claim is shown to be false.

loaded question
Asking a question that has an assumption built into it so that it can't be answered without appearing guilty.

tu quoque
Avoiding having to engage with criticism by turning it back on the accuser - you answer criticism with criticism.

ambiguity
Using double meanings or ambiguities of language to mislead or misrepresent the truth.

the gambler's fallacy
Believing that 'runs' occur to statistically independent phenomena such as roulette wheel spins.

bandwagon
Appealing to popularity or the fact that many people do something as an attempted form of validation.

burden of proof
Saying that the burden of proof lies not with the person making the claim, but with someone else to disprove.

genetic
Judging something good or bad on the basis of where it comes from, or from whom it comes.

black-or-white
Where two alternative states are presented as the only possibilities, when in fact more possibilities exist.

begging the question
A circular argument in which the conclusion is included in the premise.

appeal to authority
Using the opinion or position of an authority figure, or institution of authority, in place of an actual argument.

appeal to nature
Making the argument that because something is 'natural' it is therefore valid, justified, inevitable, good, or ideal.

composition / division
Assuming that what's true about one part of something has to be applied to all, or other, parts of it.

anecdotal
Using personal experience or an isolated example instead of a valid argument, especially to dismiss statistics.

no true scotsman
Making what could be called an appeal to purity as a way to dismiss relevant criticisms or flaws of an argument.

the texas sharpshooter
Cherry-picking data clusters to suit an argument, or finding a pattern to fit a presumption.

middle ground
Saying that a compromise, or middle point, between two extremes is the truth.

yourlogicalfallacy.com

Chapter 6

THE INFRASTRUCTURE
OF BELIEF

Le Bon characterized his theory as applying to "the Crowd" or the collective mind of the masses. In reality, there is no such thing as such a mind or a collective crowd thinking as one. Nevertheless, Le Bon was a master. He was the first to identify and codify the potential targets of propaganda action to be taken on the masses.

While somewhat rudimentary, he was able to capture the primal architecture that humans in community are subject to in the construction of beliefs. There are five main pillars of influence in a community that shape personal beliefs **that are stronger and more powerful than rational appeal to logic, facts, or even persuasive speech.** These five pillars make up *The Infrastructure of Belief.*

Le Bon laid bare a truly shocking discovery: that facts are tiny handmaidens to the true queens who alter public opinion. It is not hard to see why once you understand the model.

The five pillars that Le Bon uncovered are Imagination, Language, Authority, Social Pressure, and Experience, and they are extremely powerful forces within the herd or group, which enable humans to make decisions quickly and more easily without having to gather original data or to think in detail about every imaginable topic.

Each one of these pillars is hardwired into the nonrational part of the human brain. They are go-to subconscious techniques that make living in a community more manageable. So while facts might be readily available, for many, they will not function as the primary foundation of their belief structure in any given situation. This is why learned people can sometimes be just as susceptible to propaganda as the unlearned.

Some pillars, like Imagination and Language, help bind communities together like glue and should not be tampered with recklessly because they are indispensable to helping members find their place in society and maintain a hierarchy of cultural values. Concealed tampering with cultural stories amounts to sedition.

The five pillars that support a belief structure are Imagination (trust your culture), Language (trust the hierarchy of value in cultural words), Authority (trust the experts), Social Pressure (trust what others are doing and saying), and Experience (trust your eyes because seeing is believing).

In small, tight-knit and homogenous communities where mutual social interest and proximity are co-joined, this infrastructure works brilliantly.

For example, think of the nuclear family. Children are surrounded in a microcosm of trust. Embedded within that enclave, they inherently learn to trust that culture and its stories that address big questions like "Why am I here" and "What is my purpose?" [Imagination.]

As we shall see later, words encapsulate reality, and those adopted and regularly used by parents will be the lens through which children see and understand the world. Terms associated with approbation will be noted and made distinct from terms associated with praise and acceptance. Children learn these associations more or less by immersion and will not be able to extricate themselves from the grip of their power until they reach a greater level of maturity. [Language.]

They also learn and come to know through experience. Watching Dad scold an elder brother regarding an issue has powerful influence, as does simply watching how parents navigate the world at large. Children see—they imitate. [Experience].

Children also watch and learn which authorities the parents trust; priest, doctor, Uncle, or family friend? Who is it safe for them to trust in the larger world? [Authority.]

And finally, humans are endowed with a social nature primed for belonging to a larger social circle. Fitting in is much more comfortable than being different. Children watch and imitate the dominant cultural group with which they are surrounded, like extended family or interactions with a local parish or synagogue. [Social Pressure.]

Up until the advent of television and the geographical mobility afforded by revolutions in travel, this system worked well to reinforce cultural stability. Most people lived and died in the places where they were born. In fact, it is exceedingly difficult to break up a culture bonded in this way. This type of culture is maintained from the bottom up, from the lowest unit of cohesion—the family and then expanding outward to the broader social strata, like a pyramid.

The breakdown of the nuclear family, the dispersion of families geographically away from extended families and the lessening of interconnectedness or reliance on local community structures like church or social organizations have created a situation of severing modern man from the local "trusts" of the smaller communities natural to him for thousands of years. The word "trusts" is used purposefully.

As was mentioned earlier, the true queens of influence are these five pillars. Ignore them at your peril. A belief structure set in place by these five will take a legion of facts to dislodge, and even that might fail.

With the bottom of the pyramid now weakened, the masses have been submerged in a technological environment that has largely displaced local influence. The words used to talk about reality, the cultural stories shared, the lived experiences, the admired social networks and the experts are largely drawn from television, Hollywood, the news and public education. This has made many frightfully susceptible to disruption of what had previously been stable personal and, more importantly, cultural beliefs—through outside influences.

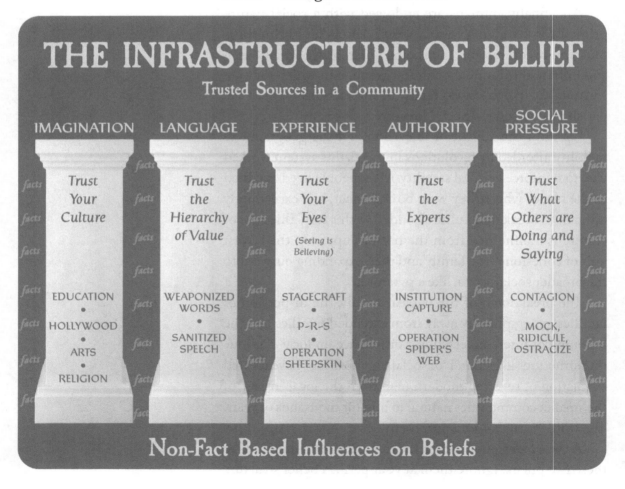

THE INFRASTRUCTURE OF BELIEF
Trusted Sources in a Community

IMAGINATION	LANGUAGE	EXPERIENCE	AUTHORITY	SOCIAL PRESSURE
Trust Your Culture	Trust the Hierarchy of Value	Trust Your Eyes (Seeing is Believing)	Trust the Experts	Trust What Others are Doing and Saying
EDUCATION • HOLLYWOOD • ARTS • RELIGION	WEAPONIZED WORDS • SANITIZED SPEECH	STAGECRAFT • P-R-S • OPERATION SHEEPSKIN	INSTITUTION CAPTURE • OPERATION SPIDER'S WEB	CONTAGION • MOCK, RIDICULE, OSTRACIZE

Non-Fact Based Influences on Beliefs

It is frightful for this reason: that modern man no longer has any way to vet or verify the "trusts" with which he is surrounded and profoundly influenced.

Savvy practitioners who manipulate *The Infrastructure of Belief* for their own ends know that propaganda is NOT an operation of logic. Let me repeat: propaganda is NOT an operation of logic or reason, and those who think otherwise have already been defeated. Modern propaganda works insidiously through the pillars of influence we have been hardwired to trust.

Let's break down these pillars further. Each pillar represents one trust in a group of trusts we have come to call culture. Imagination is the stories, myths and great ideas we come to trust; Language leads us to trust the hierarchy of value in words; Authority is the trust we place in experts; Social Pressure is the trust we place in what others are doing and saying around us; and, finally, Experience is simply trusting your eyes because seeing is believing.

IMAGINATION (TRUST YOUR CULTURE)
Education | Hollywood | Art | Music

Captivating the imagination is one of the main objectives behind most of the media today. The power of the mind to imagine through pictures, myths, symbols, and stories is profound. Le Bon correctly identified crowds or the mass mind as being susceptible to imagination ignited through the arts and entertainment. One could bypass reason and inject powerful ideas into the national consciousness as an end to the local gatekeepers of culture. Indeed, "to know the art of impressing the imagination of crowds is to know at the same time the art of governing them."[54] Le Bon is alluding to the fact that cultural stories inform political structure. The late Andrew

54. Le Bon, 37.

Breitbart echoed that sentiment with the phrase, "politics is downstream from culture."

The massive coliseums of Rome were used as a distraction from the deep divisions and civil war that had emerged following emperor Nero's suicide. The amphitheater, which housed fifty thousand spectators, was a "gift" to the people from the new emperor, Vespasian, who wasted no time in distracting the masses via a state-sponsored spectacle lasting one hundred days, providing entertainment and catharsis through bloody and brutal battle reenactments, executions and death as a substitute for violent uprisings.

Embodied in the spectacle was the theatrical version of the populace's dependence on the all-powerful state.

Another historical example is the use of motion pictures by the Office of War Information's Bureau of Motion Pictures (BMP). The BMP was established in collaboration with Hollywood in order to produce films that advanced America's aims during World War II. Some of the feature films that were used included *Sergeant York* (1941), *Bataan* (1943), *Thirty Seconds Over Tokyo* (1944), *The Story of G.I. Joe* (1945), and *They Were Expendable* (1945).

According to Elmer Davis, director of the Office of War Information:

> *The easiest way to inject a propaganda idea into most people's minds is to let it go through the medium of an entertainment picture when **they do not realize that they are being propagandized.**[55]*

Bernays also chimed in, "The American motion picture is the greatest unconscious carrier of propaganda in the world today. It is a great distributor for ideas and opinions."[56]

55. http://marb.kennesaw.edu/hollywoodandwar/exhibits/show/hollywood goestowar/censorship/owiandbmp.
56. Bernays, *Propaganda*, 166.

Current research (2017) shows that military intelligence agencies have influenced more than 1,800 films and TV shows since 2005, making Hollywood a propaganda machine for the US national security state.[57]

Most leaders in the early 1900s considered the subconscious infusion of an idea into mainstream culture through arts and entertainment to be an easy and opportune way to influence the masses. Twenty-first-century practitioners have not altered this philosophy one wit.

The tools of imagination creatively answer the question, "What should I like or value?" The great ideas in society that fuel convictions, excite passions, expand horizons and for people of faith, ignite a holy imagination, are dramatically depicted to powerful effect, and play profound roles in the shaping of daily beliefs and opinions. Take, for example, tragedy as a literary form that has fallen out of favor. A tragedy is a genre in which the hero is brought down by his own flaws. Its pathos and power rest on the noble life as the ideal and the waywardness of man to reach that ideal. This type of literary or theatrical presentation serves as a cultural conscience and a reminder to love superior things.

Cultural stories can be hijacked to serve corporate, political, and national interests that are at odds with cultural tradition and popular sentiment. Media, especially movies, music, art, entertainment, and TV, can be used to undermine a refined or elevated imagination through stories that promote selfish, materialistic passions of "the good life" depicted as a beautiful spouse, a new car, or living in a big house. Flooding the media with envy, violence, anger, and consumerism can easily displace higher level pursuits that enrich community. As Weaver says, "the modern world is creating an ideology whose hero is the satisfied consumer."[58]

57. Peter Phillips, *Giants: The Global Power Elite*, (New York, 2018), 274.
58. Ted Smith, ed., *In Defense of Tradition: Collected Shorter Writings of Richard Weaver*, 1929–1963, (Indiana, 2000), 376.

While innovations, imagination and new stories are needed from time to time to revive and refresh stagnant cultures, it does not negate the obvious danger to Western cultural values if two of the five "trusts" are in the hands of a small minority of media owners who are positioned to undermine Western values like respect for the nuclear family, belief in God, the sanctity of marriage, etc. Indeed, as observed over the historical timeline of television, it is indisputable that the selection of topics has had an overall subversive and corrosive effect on the hierarchy of values traditionally espoused by the West.

LANGUAGE
(TRUST THE HIERARCHY OF VALUE IN CULTURAL WORDS)

In Chapter 9, we will be discussing at length the concepts of using language as a cultural weapon and opinion-shaper. There are four specific ways in which language can be corrupted: let's categorize them as wars; the "War over Definition," the "War over Direction," the "War over Relations, and the "War over Reality." For now, we'll look at some basic concepts in each category.

Ivy Lee, a publicity agent for the Pennsylvania Railroad and a contemporary of Bernays, expounded in a speech to the American Railway Guild on the art of "getting believed in." Lee counseled would-be practitioners on the critical importance of word choice. For example, if one was opposing a "full crew" law, the name of the measure should be changed to the "extra crew" law and continually referred to as such.

Going through a "bankruptcy?" Call it a "readjustment of finances." If a small group of strikers is demanding a particularly high wage increase, make it appear that all miners are asking for a hundred and fifty percent increase in wages.[59] With the mere choice of words, Lee was able to frame the labor "requests" as "unreasonable demands." The story to which the public will respond is altered, in some ways, outright falsified through omission, exaggeration or lack of candor.

This is a War over Definition and is played out in the public relations efforts on both sides of most prominent issues. Are people who want to regulate or restrict abortions anti-abortionists or pro-lifers?

Are those for unrestricted access to abortions pro-choice or anti-life? The central issue is framing the narrative, pinning the tail on the donkey or the enemy right at the start. The public should not be allowed to come to their own conclusions—spell them out through word choice at the outset of discussion.

The "War over Reality" can be found when older words are discreetly replaced with newer terms that quietly undermine or displace the current cultural reality. At times, the process by which this is accomplished can be undertaken with little interference and virtually unnoticed by the citizenry. After all, it's only a word.

The current push to replace terms that end in man (policeman, fireman, spokesman) with gender-neutral substitutes (police officer, firefighter and spokesperson) may appear innocuous or benign but, in fact, they are and should be viewed as a serious provocation to the old order that views gender as stable and immutable and holds to the historical convention of the English language usage of the term "man" to include all human beings.

In 2018, the New York state legislature passed a bill that would codify the use of gender-neutral terms like firefighter

59. Upton Sinclair, *The Brass Check: A Study of American Journalism, Evidence and Reasons Behind The Media's Corruption*, (France, 1919), 225.

and police officer in all future state laws, a change that seemed innocuous at the time. A mere three years later, laws were changed to allow a gender neutral option on a birth certificate marking a tectonic cultural shift. Pay attention when new terms are introduced into the lexicon.

A corollary to this idea is the importance of seeking and staking out working definitions of vague and nebulous words thrown about recklessly by politicians in order to play on the emotions and sentiments of the populace. Frequently, they are using powerful terms like "democracy," "social justice," and "equality" but have functionally defined those terms in a different way than is commonly used. Many take for granted that those potentially different meanings are one and the same.

The right word spoken at the right time with the right tone to move people in the right direction is what is defined in the classic study of rhetoric. The art of moving men's passions in pursuit of a goal, that is the art of rhetorical speech. It seeks to compel men to action. This is the "War over Direction."

The gutting of rhetoric, its study as a serious academic discipline, and its use in society is yet another way that the correct use of language has been disabled and disarmed. Scientific language has been idolized, and passionate rhetoric has been disparaged in the cultural square. Ever since World War II, rhetoric has been disingenuously maligned as being synonymous with propaganda—a casualty of Hitler's success.

Persuasive language that points mankind to the highest good is a revolutionary force that is in desperate need of revival in order to re-awaken citizens who have been lulled to sleep by scientifically sanitized speech and "polite" business-style conversation.

Finally, the greatest attack on language is censorship and this must be resisted at every level. You cannot have a free society without free speech, period. Any attempt to argue that others must be protected from offense and hurt feelings should be utterly repudiated. No government, no company, no fact-checkers can ever be the arbiters of truth.

Ideas and their spread are revolutionary. To arms with words!

EXPERIENCE (TRUST YOUR EYES: SEEING IS BELIEVING)

Stagecraft / Operation Sheepskin

Experience gives us tangible information about the world, allowing us to draw conclusions quickly from our surroundings and take action. Experience is the epicenter of the model because it is such a strong persuader. "Seeing is believing" is not just a meaningless phrase. Sight orients us to what we perceive as reality.

Another way to explain the power of experience or events is to expose the truth behind well-known phrases such as "show, don't tell," "seeing is believing," and "I'm just not seeing it."

A parent is told of conflict between two siblings, but he is not convinced that the situation is really serious. When one child returns to the house with a bloody nose as a result of the situation, the parent now "sees it." It becomes an active problem that must now be managed. Such is the effect of real, live events on the mind of the public.

In the age of mass communication, "local" community experiences compete with shared so-called media "experiences" that are witnessed through the lens of the news media. Repetition and dissemination of these media "experiences "magnify their effects exponentially.

Stagecraft, the masterful trademark technique of Edward Bernays (discussed in Chapter 4), is simply the manipulation of the pillar of Experience in the service of government, politicians, and corporations in order to shape beliefs and create demand.

This concept will be developed more fully in Chapter 7 when "Operation Sheepskin as a Tool" is fully introduced.

AUTHORITY (TRUST THE EXPERTS)

Institution Capture / Operation Spider's Web

Authority is an honor bestowed upon members of the community deserving of respect, whether for acts of heroism, for their learned wisdom, or for their judgment in leadership. They have earned the right to be heard and their opinions respected. In a small community, these people are generally known personally and deemed to be people of high character whose words match their behavior and who can be trusted.

Most people don't have time to research everything they need to know in order to make informed decisions. The first impulse of the public in making up its mind is to follow the example of a trusted leader. This is one of the most firmly established principles of mass psychology. "If you can influence the leaders, either with or without their conscious cooperation, you automatically influence the group which they sway."[60]

A historical example of this is the recruitment of prominent local leaders by the Creel Committee in World War I to become Four Minute Men. The Four Minute Men were trained to give four-minute speeches intended to influence friends and citizens in their community who respected and admired them in order to support the war effort. In this way, Creel and other government lackeys hijacked the trust accorded to local authorities and used it in the service of war propaganda.

The use of doctors as spokesmen for tobacco companies during the 1900s to promote smoking is yet another example of how trusted leaders could lend credibility and support to a narrative: "Smoking doesn't harm you, even doctors smoke."

Respect for the opinions of celebrities, whether rightly earned or not, does hold weight for certain segments of the population, and their popularity does get utilized in support for issues or causes as needed.

60. Ibid, 73.

Symbols of authority are now more distant, inaccessible, and more easily manipulated in a mass culture. Titles and positions usually signal authority, but as observed through the camera lens, who can say whether this authority is genuine? The media is supposed to be vetting authorities, but are they?

The Elizabeth O'Bagy story is part of my own personal odyssey of learning to vet "distant, made-for-TV authorities."

The Elizabeth O'Bagy Story

FOX news anchor Brett Baer introduced a special in-studio guest—a supposed Syrian expert confidently suggesting that U.S. officials should arm the rebels because they were mostly moderates and not fanatics. Common sense told me that this woman, who was relatively young, late twenties or early thirties, was not likely to be a Syrian expert because of her youth and the cultural views that Middle Easterners generally hold toward women. Her unusual name, Elizabeth O'Bagy, caught my attention and the unusual name of the organization that she represented, "The Institute for the Study of War," stood out.

Armed with my suspicions, I confirmed that The Institute for the Study of War was a hawkish Washington non-profit whose leadership consisted of ex-military personnel and that the majority of its funding was from the military-industrial complex, including CACI Ever Vigilant, General Dynamics, and ManTech International Corporation, to name a few.

Questioning Secretary of State John Kerry during a September 3 hearing on Syria, Senator John McCain read extensively from a Wall Street Journal op-ed by "Dr. Elizabeth O'Bagy" about the growing moderate Syrian opposition. The next day, testifying before a House committee, Kerry himself cited O'Bagy's work in explaining how only 15% to 20% of the 70,000 to 100,000 fighters on the ground in Syria were "bad guys."

Dr. Elizabeth O'Bagy, cited as a venerated Syria expert by some of the highest officials in America, was in reality a fledgling researcher sent to Syria a scant 20 months earlier as an intern with The Institute. Weeks after she had come to my attention, she was dismissed from the Institute for resume-padding, claiming to have obtained a doctorate from Georgetown University.

Intense scrutiny into her background by the truth seekers in alternative media ultimately had been triggered by the Wall Street Journal op-ed piece and led to her dismissal from the Institute. It was also revealed that she failed to disclose a secondary job she held with the Syrian Emergency Task Force, a Washington lobby group advocating for the armed overthrow of the government of Syria.

Less than two weeks after her fall from grace, the ultimate war hawk himself, John McCain, softened her harsh landing by appointing her as a legislative assistant in his Washington DC office.

O'Bagy's media appearances were not limited to Fox News. She had in fact received widespread exposure on numerous media outlets such as CNN, MSNBC, PBS, and NPR, just to name a few.

That a 26-year-old without vetted credentials and scant Syrian expertise became a media starlet, delivered speeches at universities and think tanks, briefed over fourteen

Senate and twenty House officials and was quoted by high-ranking senior American officials at congressional hearings is a profoundly disturbing phenomenon and a striking example of propaganda in the heart of the American political system.

If we reverse engineer this bizarre story, we find a discomforting scenario of events.

Elizabeth O'Bagy, young, attractive, and well-spoken, was heralded as neutral (Institute for the Study of War) and exploited to support the ousting of Assad as an agenda promoted by powers much greater than herself.

She accompanied John McCain and his entourage to Syria and, voila, she became a newly minted expert farmed out to the various media outlets.

Which brings us to the question of vetting authorities by media outlets on both the right and the left. Is it likely that each and every media outlet was guilty of a singular instance of bad judgment, or lax standards? Was there an epic failure by numerous institutions and individuals on both sides of the political aisle to vet the credentials of the same person? What are the odds?

The media, the Secretary of State, a prominent senator, and our government-funded NGOs were all co-conspirators in promoting "experts' and pedaling illusions of reality with the intent to deceive the average American.

Isn't it evident that the media, in collusion with the American government, purposefully attempted to deceive the American people?

Ron Paul's response to this fiasco was to point out O'Bagy's financial support through an NGO (Non-Governmental Organizations) the Syrian Emergency Task Force was directly tied to the America government itself. Not only were we lied to about Syria, we were forced to pay for the privilege.

The O'Bagy Story Raises Profound Questions

The breakdown of O'Bagy's story, including the finances and the players who promoted and facilitated her rise to stardom, is a fascinating study on the inner workings of the contemporary propaganda machine. Elizabeth O'Bagy was ultimately a propaganda puppet in the service of powerful elites, facilitating her entry into and manipulating her circulation among the most celebrated media establishments.

Two shocking takeaways from this story emerge: more proof that the media is engaged in something other than simply reporting the news in an unbiased fashion and that creating "experts" is part of a larger strategy of manufacturing opinion and steering the masses to predetermined ends.

SOCIAL PRESSURE
(TRUST WHAT OTHERS ARE DOING AND SAYING)

Contagion or social proof is the failsafe where a man, unsure of his conviction, looks around to see what other people think and modulates his response or opinion as a result. "Should this product, idea, or cause be valued?" is the relevant question, and the search for an easy answer can be found in the majority opinion, favorable reviews, or glowing news reports.

This taps into the deep psychological need to be a part of a group and to belong—as opposed to being a lone voice standing apart from the crowd. Rejection and/or ostracism is painful and uncomfortable for most people, and the fear of it can cause the average person to follow along meekly, afraid to swim upstream against the current of accepted thinking.

A folktale written by Hans Christian Anderson in 1837, *The Emperor's New Clothes*, highlights the power of social pressure. Two swindlers disguised as weavers look to capitalize on the King's vanity and his lavish spending on clothes. They offer to supply him with magnificent clothes that are invisible to those who are stupid or incompetent. His trusted advisors play along with the charade, not wanting to appear stupid or unfit for their role.

The townspeople, aware that the clothes are invisible to those who are stupid and incompetent, go along with the pretense until finally, oblivious to the social sanction, a young child blurts out, "The emperor has no clothes." While this story can be used to highlight the vanity of the King, it is also illustrative of the lengths people will go to avoid public ridicule.

Unfortunately, most people cannot break free from what they perceive to be the overwhelming weight of social evidence in order to think independently and make up their own minds about issues and events, especially when doing so will get them tarred and feathered in the court of public opinion.

To the extent that culture is largely imposed nationally versus locally, it is very difficult to resist the "surround sound" of orthodoxy induced by a collaboration of the five pillars.

It is easy to see why rational thought by itself is not an infallible bulwark against the capture and subversion of the five columns that comprise the Infrastructure of Belief. These mechanisms are shortcuts to knowledge as well as opinions in small local communities that have been hacked and put to use by sophisticated forces in order to broadly manipulate opinions and beliefs in a technologically shaped culture.

The collective power of the five columns to stimulate massive social pressure can easily overwhelm the individual into thinking, "Everyone thinks this way," or "Everyone is doing this." Caught in isolation, many people retreat even from previous tightly held beliefs. For the few that resist, the majority can reject and ostracize them. Such is the raging antipathy toward those who do not conform.

SUMMARY

There are five main pillars of influence in a community that shape personal beliefs **that are stronger and more powerful than rational appeal to logic, facts, or even persuasive speech.** These five pillars make up *The Infrastructure of Belief*.

Comprehending these social dynamics is one of the main keys to understanding the pervasiveness of modern-day propaganda. It would be easy if all we had to do were to identify the "Big Lie."

The five pillars in *The Infrastructure of Belief*:

1. Imagination (Trust Your Culture)

2. Language (Trust the Hierarchy of Value in Cultural Words)

3. Experience (Trust Your Eyes: Seeing Is Believing)

4. Authority (Trust the Experts)

5. Social Pressure (Trust What Others Are Doing and Saying)

The Infrastructure of Belief keeps mankind culturally integrated and somewhat naturally conformist. A brilliant adaptation in small local communities where each one of these trusts can be tried and tested. In a mass technological world, the potential to infuse and cleave ideas from the top down into a weakened base by misusing the trusts that man has acquired over millennium is like kryptonite.

The identification of these pillars and how they are manipulated in Chapters 7, 8 and 9 will enable us to begin the process of reverse engineering a breakaway.

In the next chapter, I'll introduce the concept of "Operation Sheepskin," its foundational centerpiece; the manipulation of experience and the primal brain responses to unknown territory that allow it to forcefully and powerfully drive change that benefits the propagandist.

Chapter 7

OPERATION SHEEPSKIN

DANVILLE, VIRGINIA

Some ten years ago, my job took me to Danville, Virginia. I looked forward to spending time in a quiet southern Virginia town. Much to my surprise and dismay, Danville was filled with a sense of hopelessness and despair, the origins of which I could hardly fathom. On a hill near the river, turn-of-the-century architectural masterpieces had transformed into rat-infested blight. As I drove the countryside, abandoned tobacco smokehouses dotted the landscape, relics of a bygone era of economic prosperity. I left Danville with lingering questions as to what caused the economic collapse of this once vibrant town.

Ten years later, while researching for this book, I came across a six-part series of articles on the railroad trusts by Ray Stannard Baker published in McClure's magazine in 1906, including this piece: *The Way of a Railroad with a Town; Story of the Struggle of Danville, Virginia with the Southern Railway*, which tells the story of corporate corruption through monopolistic consolidation and rate fixing—the practice of offering discount railroad rates to select groups like the tobacco trusts and owners of the corporate mills on the Dan River but not to the people at large or small businesses.

City leaders made several futile attempts to foster more competition by raising funds for a competing railroad line. In one case, the Southern Railroad simply bought it out and regained the monopoly and in another case, they operated at a loss until the smaller railroad went out of business. The city leaders, in exasperation, took their case to the Interstate Commerce Commission, who ruled in their favor not once but twice and yet failed to gain any relief from the Southern Railroad to alter their rates. In the end, Danville was forced to use more city money to sue Southern Railway in an attempt to obtain justice. The court ruled in favor of the railroad.

Years later, adding insult to injury, the manufacturing interests fled overseas to take advantage of cheap labor. The beautiful turn-of-the-century homes that had housed the benefactors of the railroad's special rates were sold, leaving the town destitute of economic viability. Ten years later, I had my answers; a valiant battle with economic pirates had been fought and lost.[61]

HAVING YOUR CAKE AND EATING IT TOO

In a separate article, Baker outlined another endeavor embarked upon by the owners of Southern Railroad at the turn of the century, an operation to remake public opinion—or operation "putting lipstick on a pig." A small publicity agency out of Boston, MA was hired and, in turn, quickly opened multiple offices in Chicago, Washington, St. Louis, and Topeka,

---

61. Ray Stannard Baker, *The Way of a Railroad with a Town; Story of the Struggle of Danville, Virginia with the Southern Railway in McClures, (New York, 1906), Vol 27.*

Kansas, employing agents working in distant locations like South Dakota and California.

The agency created a system of analyzing and modifying public opinion by examining each and every newspaper for articles touching upon the railroad. Railroad agents were sent out to each and every paper for the purpose of creating a file or dossier on its editor, recording his political and religious leanings, views on the trust issue, the industrial and commercial make-up of the town and so forth. It was a massive undertaking.

Armed with this knowledge, well-written articles designed to appeal to country editors were made freely available for print but which also contained masked material favorable to the railroads. Weeks later, re-examination of the papers revealed how many of the articles were used and in what format. Ultimately, this process was named "The Barometer" for its ability to gauge the amount of favorable and unfavorable public sentiment percolating at large across the country, an early forerunner of public opinion polling. Baker recounted that in one state alone, Nebraska, the unfavorable to favorable article ratio was transformed from a dismal 212 to 2 against into 202 to 4 in favor after an eleven-week campaign.

For simplicity's sake, I've portrayed the rise of corporate propaganda as occurring after WWI. In fact, The Boston Publicity Bureau (1905) was the first organized company created for the purpose of changing public opinion in the United States. At the turn of the century, there was great clamoring for the Trusts to be broken apart or, worse yet, be converted to public agencies in order to curb abuses.

So great was the need to repair Southern Railway's disastrous reputation—justly earned through prolonged predatory monopolistic practices—that even the use of novice practitioners in a rudimentary new propaganda technique at great expense made complete sense.

So while the "wolf" was pilfering and plundering local communities, he very much desired to appear sheeplike. This statement probably comes as close to anything to being the essence of propaganda. It is the age-old story of deceit and betrayal straight from the Garden.

OPERATION SHEEPSKIN EXPLAINED

The "Wolf," however, is not content. Sniffing the wind, he senses other opportunities beyond rehabilitating tarnished reputations, selling products, and steering public opinion to favor public policy options or even supporting a war.

After all, why not be a bit more proactive considering all the technological tools now available? You can hardly blame him for thinking big. Why not work together with other wolves and steer the big ship of public opinion straight into piles of profits for us and our friends? Tell the sheep a story. Get them worked up and a tad nervous and disoriented, and then lead them to safety. We'll look great . . . "Like my new sheepskin?" AND rake in tons of cash.

As a type of shorthand and as a reminder of its deceptive nature, let's name this type of organized campaign "Operation Sheepskin."

Operation sheepskin represents an elevation in scope and cooperation from the previous techniques discussed. This is not a lone wolf operation; it requires a pack of wolves, a cabal of sorts working together for clandestine reasons.

At the center of this campaign is a cover or meta-story to mask the hidden agenda. Essentially this is the alchemy or art of propaganda. The meta-story is a problem or issue which is dramatically revealed to the community that must be solved by a benevolent and disinterested source, usually the government. Words are selected that frame the story from the start, and authorities are marshaled in support.

The news media, functioning as the de facto tribal elders of the technological society, uncover a dangerous problem with potential to harm the community. Alarms are sent out far and wide, cue up the smoke signals and usher in the counsel. The so-called elders are now in position to sanction and validate the story while steering the options for resolution.

Gabriel Tarde, a contemporary of Le Bon, in *The Laws of Imitation* (1890; English translation 1903), stressed that the selection of topics available in the news for any given day determined largely what conversations occurred, such that even those who failed to read the news were "forced to follow the groove of their borrowed thoughts. One pen suffices to set off a million tongues."[62]

Lippmann likened the press to the beam of a searchlight moving restlessly about "bringing one episode and then another out of darkness and into vision."[63] Selection of one problem over another by "bringing it to light" awakens public consciousness causing agitation for a resolution. Ignoring an issue in the press keeps the public ignorant and uninformed but doesn't lessen the potential danger of inattentiveness.

What I've classified as the tribal eldership of the news media is no small thing. Problems that go unaddressed for years can suddenly rise to the surface having become much larger and more formidable than in their infancy. In a similar vein, focusing on ill-conceived distractions and ignoring the truly important can be as calamitous. This oft-ignored power to set the agenda of the public square is akin to the sacred role of a tribal eldership whose wisdom is critical to protect and lead. Control of the eldership in the wrong hands is disastrous.

62. Jonathan Auerbach, *Weapons of Democracy: Propaganda, Progressivism, And American Public Opinion*, (Maryland, 2015), 29.
63. Walter Lippmann, *Public Opinion*, (Virginia, 2010), 197.

GUATEMALA

Now is a good time to get back to our friend Mr. Bernays to examine a large-scale campaign involving much more serious consequences and coordination than simple stagecraft.

In March 1951, an action to seize British oil properties by the Iranian government prompted Bernays to write a letter warning United Fruit's publicity chief Edmund Whitman that immediate action should be taken to secure against a similar attempt at expropriation of United Fruit properties by Guatemala in the future.

United Fruit had been operating in the country for over eighty years. They virtually owned the small country, hence the term "Banana Republic," a pejorative term coined with Guatemala in mind.

Seventy percent of the land was owned by 7% of the population. They owned most of the railroad, had significant control of the only Atlantic seaport, paid no taxes, were the largest land-owner, employer and exporter and had a guarantee that workers be paid no more than 50 cents a day. "It was a capitalist dream."[64]

Into that unseemly history arose Juan Jose Arevalo, a professor living in exile in Argentina. Following an uprising to oust the military General Jorge Ubico Castaneda, Arevalo was swept into office. He began to make small changes to create a democratic system and grant the workers the right to protect their interests. He was succeeded in March 1951, the same year as the Iranian seizure of British Oil, by Jacobo Arbenz Guzman, who dreamed of even grander plans to help his people.

Between 1952 and 1954, he introduced legislation that would expropriate 1.5 million acres of uncultivated lands with repayment in government bonds to be redistributed to the poorest families of Guatemala for cultivation. At risk for United

64. Larry Tye, *The Father of Spin: Edward L. Bernays And The Birth of Public Relations*, (New York, 1998), 166.

Fruit was not only the loss of hundreds of thousands of acres but, more importantly, a staggering loss of political control.

Two years before the land expropriations started, Bernays, who served as public relations counsel for United Fruit, recommended a media blitz that would place articles in magazines that had broad readership, including the New York Times, the New York Herald Tribune, The Atlantic Monthly, Time, Newsweek and others all centered on the growing threat of Communism in Guatemala. He also recommended that the company hire a noteworthy Latin American official who would condemn expropriation; a top international lawyer who could set forth the legal reasons condemning it and to convince a top university to hold a conference on how America should respond to such actions.

As a result of Bernays's work, the story of deplorable pro-communist conditions and the potential dangers at hand now circulated in the public consciousness. He counseled United Fruit that the next action steps should be bold and include lobbying for a change in the US ambassador, the imposition of congressional sanctions against government aid to pro-communist regimes and finally, the subsidization of research by disinterested groups like the Brookings Institute into the sociopolitical details of the conflict.[65]

In January 1952, Bernays invited influential reporters to the country on a two-week all-expense paid junket to see the communist threat firsthand. Although Bernays would swear reporters were free to come and go as they wished, Thomas McCann, a young PR official for United Fruit, alleged years later in his memoirs that everything was carefully staged and controlled to compromise objectivity.

Earlier on, Bernays repositioned Guatemala and United Fruit as located in "Middle America" because it had a more

65. Ibid, 168.

wholesome feel to it than Central America, and he had created the "Middle America Information Bureau," which distributed literature and stories to interested journalists in the United States and other foreign nations as well as published The Latin American Report weekly geared to businessmen. All literature was approved by United Fruit.

In 1953, Eisenhower had replaced Truman, a man he criticized as being soft on communism. And by October 19th Rudolf Schoenfeld, US ambassador to Guatemala who resisted attempts to classify Arbenz as a threat, had been replaced with Jack Peurifoy, just as Bernays had recommended months earlier.

There were other important administration changes; John Foster Dulles, a former lawyer for United Fruit, was appointed Secretary of State, and John Cabot, whose brother had briefly served as president of United Fruit, was appointed assistant Secretary of State for Latin American Affairs. Allen Dulles, Foster's brother was already head of the CIA. Peurifoy wasted no time putting international pressure on the Guatemalan government. On his first trip, he fired a loaded question at members of the government demanding, "When was Guatemala going to stop being a bridgehead for Communism?"

In August 1953, Eisenhower had authorized the CIA to implement Operation Success, a mission to overthrow the democratically elected government of Guatemala. The fix was in while efforts to isolate the country internationally continued at the conference of the Organization of American States in Caracas, Venezuela, in March 1954.

Costa Rica refused to attend in protest. Delegates complained that all efforts by Guatemala for economic independence were being categorized and mislabeled as subversive "Communism." A vote was finally taken in favor of "positive action" against Guatemala, no doubt influenced by Dulles' suggestion that US aid could be withdrawn if the Latin countries refused.

On June 18, 1954, a CIA-backed rebel force led by Carlos Castillo Armas, who was later installed as Guatemala's military dictator, "stormed" the capital and toppled the Arbenz government, causing him and his family to flee the country.

On behalf of United Fruit, the United States government would argue that United Fruit had been subject to a "virtual" expropriation, a term crafted by Bernays, and theft because the Guatemalan government had paid for the land with the artificially low land valuation that United Fruit had conveniently used for years to avoid tax and because they paid in bonds and not in cash.

Arbenz and his family, hounded for years by the CIA, were never allowed back to Guatemala. Nations that granted them asylum were subject to recriminations and threats by United States personnel, and they fled from country to country, looking for a home. Six years after the suicide of his daughter at age twenty-five, Arbenz was found dead in a bathtub filled with scalding water in a Mexico City hotel, a supposed suicide. He was fifty-seven.

The country of Guatemala entered a 36-year civil war that claimed the lives of an estimated 200,000 civilians. Much more is known about this incident than could be recounted here in this brief summary.

This story brings up a host of difficult questions. If only it were a stand-alone story, it would be easier to dismiss. But the coup that brought down the Shah of Iran bears similar marks. Naomi Klein, in her New York Times bestseller, *The Shock Doctrine: The Rise of Disaster Capitalism*, recounts story after story of intervention by the United States in foreign countries under the pretense of liberation that ends up looking more like a license to steal for capitalists leaving a reign of terror in the wake of the heist.

In 1956, C. Wright Mills, a sociologist and author of The *Power Elite*, wrote that America was ruled by those who control the "strategic command posts" of society—big corporations, the machinery of the state, and the military establishment. For most readers, this is the hardest mental bridge to cross. Is there an invisible government? A cabal of wolves hiding behind a veneer of democracy? Everything in your mind and heart tells you, "No, it can't be so." I certainly don't expect you to believe it because I said it. You must investigate for yourself. The recommended reading at the back of the book is a good place to start.

CONCEPTUAL MODEL

The basic outline of Operation Sheepskin looks like this:

Mission: Create a meta-story consisting of problem-reaction-solution that can be narrated and dramatized to the desired audience. In accepting the solution to the story, the public is forced to swallow the hidden agenda that is not in their interests.

The Campaign: Implement an event or, more frequently, a sequence of events that can be manufactured to dramatize the issue to the public. This should evoke some type of worry or anxiety to draw attention. Mobilize experts and authorities who highlight the problem and give insight on multiple solutions.

> *Events work like a primer or ignition switch to pique interest, capture attention, generate emotion, create fear and anxiety. Remember, experience is one of the most powerful pillars in The Infrastructure of Belief, and fear is the most powerful emotion for driving change.*

The Press: The press functions as tribal elders highlighting and magnifying the importance of the manufactured events and sanctioning the wisdom of authorities to address the problem. The press sets the narrative or storyline of the event and/or frames the issue that needs to be resolved in the midst of competing alternatives. Should an undesirable alternative gain traction, their job is to discredit either the alternative or the person who holds that position.

The Solution: The solution always encompasses the hidden agenda and includes a myriad of societal modifications, including legislative changes, allocation of government funds for stealth projects, transformation of government structure, policy changes that benefit insiders, and finally, the declaration of a steady stream of phony "wars." Wars are a very useful tactic, as many critics of culture and society have noted. Declarations of war have been pronounced continuously over the past 75 years against everything from drugs, foreign despots, cancer, violence, viruses, and the nebulous war on poverty.

The centerpiece for most of these so-called wars is the passage of comprehensive legislation—the impact of which is largely unintelligible to average citizens without a room full of lawyers. Legislative packages, often written months or years prior to a campaign, have slim to no chance of being passed in normal times. However, they are able to garner support after the pathogenic priming of the population with fear, indignation or revenge—all being incredibly strong emotions that can render sheep compliant and susceptible.

Nothing galvanizes the imagination and emotions of a population more than a war or a "holy crusade" against real or imagined enemies.

Operation Sheepskin is the tool through which new laws, policy, and "wars" are justified in the public mind. The power of a coordinated campaign can force major cultural change even in the face of significant resistance.

Operation Sheepskin illustrates how imagination (the story over facts) experience (the issue made real) language (essential for framing the narrative) and authority (experts who know what to do); four main pillars in the Infrastructure of Belief undergird the campaign with the fifth pillar in play as the narrative reaches critical mass (Social Pressure/Social Contagion).

Lather, rinse, and repeat for social policy, money allocation, legislation, and even wars thought helpful to increasing monopolies of cash and power.

The existence of rats in a home is most frequently revealed by observing the droppings. The cabal's main goal is to remain out of sight, unobserved and hidden to the casual observer. The droppings are another story entirely.

Knowledge of the patterns; a cast of common characters; the deceptive use of words to distort, confuse and misrepresent; the orchestration of events and their timing; the obviousness of the one grand narrative and the presence of "contrived" authorities begin to announce themselves to your senses. Rejoice that your propaganda radar is working.

This does not mean that you will instantly pick up on the hidden agenda, as that may take time and some digging to uncover, but the alarm has been sounded, and you are becoming streetwise and foolproof.

PRIMAL BRAIN ARCHITECTURE

Understanding primal brain architecture will reveal why experience is such a powerful tool in shaping public opinion. You'll be able to understand and identify what constitutes a noteworthy event and why. And how those events can be ratcheted up to greater and greater effect.

On a very basic level, the world can be separated into two simple categories: known and unknown territory.

Known territory is composed of familiar surroundings, people, events and even culture; a place of safety where you know how to act and what to expect from others. Unknown territory is that which is not familiar. It holds the capacity for both promise and potential as well as for threat and harm.

In the animal kingdom, the existence of predators makes encountering unknown territory a scary prospect. Prey will often freeze before cautiously exploring new territory until they are satisfied that nothing is present that can harm them.

A similar pattern of behavior exists in young toddlers. Presented with a new environment, the child will cling to its mother—who represents known territory. As the child becomes more comfortable with their surroundings, curiosity rises, and he will start to explore bit by bit, but then quickly retreats back to the known (mother) if overwhelmed with too much new information or when he feels threatened.

As adults, we continue to be both interested and leery of the unknown because it holds both promise and potential harm. Unknown territory, as expressed in a society, can be categorized along a continuum from interesting to threatening and even to chaos. Effective stagecraft can be interjected at every point along that continuum. Traveling to the right on the continuum generates stronger and stronger impulses to be brought back to safety.

The presentation of relatively benign novel events, as we saw in the Torches of Freedom, stimulates interest and curiosity in the topic at hand. Alternately a campaign like Operation Gladio, bombings in Europe by the CIA that were blamed on communists, terrorized the population and succeeded in tarnishing the communist movement galvanizing anger against communist political parties in general.

The power to drive people toward desired outcomes and to manipulate them into taking specific actions unlikely under normal conditions increases with the escalation of threat.

In the following section, I'll explore these categories in more detail.

CATEGORIES OF STAGECRAFT

1. Novel

2. Disconcerting

3. Threatening

4. Non-Event

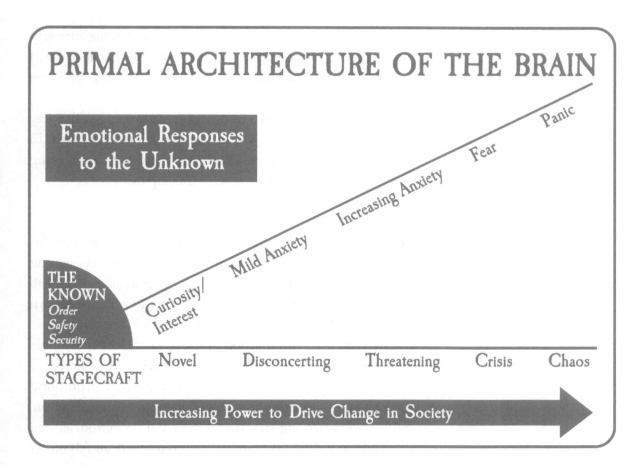

PRIMAL ARCHITECTURE OF THE BRAIN

Emotional Responses to the Unknown

Panic

Fear

Increasing Anxiety

Mild Anxiety

Curiosity/ Interest

THE KNOWN
Order
Safety
Security

TYPES OF STAGECRAFT   Novel   Disconcerting   Threatening   Crisis   Chaos

Increasing Power to Drive Change in Society

NOVEL STAGECRAFT

As we have already discussed, novel Stagecraft captures the attention, spurs opinions, and catalyzes action. This type of stagecraft involves staged events mimicking infrequent or unusual events that naturally attract attention in a community.

Think about the natural curiosity that is aroused in a local community by a rush of people dashing down the street to see the first electric car. People inherently want to know what everyone is excited about. Am I missing out on something? The manufactured events created by Bernays in the piano example were novel and interesting, drawing attention to the manufactured narrative that every home needed a music room.

Violation of social norms can cause enormous curiosity because most people confine their behavior to what is expected and socially conditioned, which is why Bernays was effective in the "Torches of Freedom" story.

Women who smoked were considered low-class. The presentation of high-class women contending for their right to smoke was definitely news. Who were these women breaking social conventions, and what were they up to?

Disagreement/Conflict

Nothing ignites attention like a disagreement. Intellectual debates may be stimulating for some people, but on a bus or subway, for example, all heads turn when disagreements arise. Who will win? Who is right? Will it escalate? The dynamics of known territory are disrupted. Many questions rush to the surface.

Bernays used this method in the political leader example to dramatize an issue, thus making it much more relevant to a wider audience. Things like staging a boycott, promoting opinions highlighting the dangers of some course of action, publicizing alarming trends and the need for action, as well as groups agitating for change or even protests all fall under this heading.

Dramatizing conflict gets the public asking questions and stimulates thinking about the validity of current practices. It also gets people to contemplate new courses of action that would have been unlikely to be considered prior to the encounter with staged disagreement.

Astroturf

"Astroturfing," a modern but related term, is event creation designed to look like an organic grassroots protest. Financial sponsors of the event, which can include paid protesters, are hidden from public view. News coverage of the event signals to the public that many people in the community are disturbed or outraged at the issue being protested when in fact, this is not the case. The paid promotional message sent to the public is, "Something needs to be done about this critical issue!"

The "predetermined ends" for which the staged event was organized could be promoted at the event or immediately after the event by political leaders so that it appears as a spontaneous solution. Meanwhile, the public has been "primed" to gullibly accept the solution that has been selected for them by the masterminds of the event.

Fake Social Media

Fake social media can be considered a subset of astroturfing. It's an attempt to create the illusion of magnified grassroots support or outrage. Hired people and automated bots that tweet, retweet, like and follow others can be used to project high volume interest in a pet issue, idea, or cause (political or otherwise). Conversely, it can be used to demoralize an opponent such that they appear to be outnumbered and ostracized by artificially inflated numbers of people holding opposing viewpoints which mimics a psychological operation on morale.

DISCONCERTING STAGECRAFT

Disconcerting Stagecraft captures attention, ignites passion, and catalyzes action but also causes low to moderate levels of anxiety and concern. It is more unsettling than novel stagecraft because there is a higher perceived threat and more unanswered questions.

Protests that turn into mobs of armed or threatening citizens roaming the streets or that are associated with the destruction of property are disconcerting when viewed on the news from a distance. Will mobs start up in my community? What will happen if they continue? Why are people angry? Will people be harmed? Can the authorities intervene? What is the solution?

Agitation

Paid disruption of any proceeding is unsettling not only to the participants but to any observers who may be watching on television. Crowds on Demand, a Beverly Hills firm, boasts that it provides clients with protests, rallies, flash mobs, paparazzi events and other inventive PR stunts. [66]

Corporations, industry organizations lobbying for change and high stakes political campaigns seeking to weigh public opinion in their favor and no longer bothered by ethics can now pay people to disrupt a rally or official proceeding. Edward Walker, a UCLA sociology professor and author of *Grassroots for Hire: Public Affairs Consultants in American Democracy*, states that "there are hundreds of lobbying firms and public affairs firms that do this work though not all in the same way."

The escalation of this technique further out the continuum toward rioting and violence fails to strain the imagination. Paid provocateurs purposefully hired to turn a peaceful event or march ugly through violence and/or rioting effectively discredit the group and its ideas.

Historically, this type of thing happened regularly with the use of Pinkerton guards hired as strike-busters during the progressive era. Agents were known to kill if necessary and lie about who initiated the violence. The press relying on witnesses and ofttimes conflicted by advertising dollars from big interests reported the lies of the Pinkertons as fact turning public opinion against the strikers.[67]

THREATENING STAGECRAFT

Threatening Stagecraft vividly captures attention and ignites one of the strongest emotions known to man, fear and its close

---

66. https://www.latimes.com/business/la-fi-crowds-extortion-20181021-story.html.
67. https://newrepublic.com/article/147619/pinkertons-still-never-sleep.

associate, anxiety. In the presence of these passions, actions are often poorly thought out and reactionary. Return to safety can dominate thinking, leading to poor choices.

Crises

No doubt, the most controversial use of this technique comes when leaders use a crisis, a natural disaster or even a tragedy like a school shooting to promote an agenda like gun control in the immediate aftermath.

In the wake of Katrina, a republican congressman, wealthy developers, and corporate lobbyists were touting that the city had finally been cleaned up and that big opportunities were around the corner. Savvy residents understood the euphuism of "a safer, smaller city" meant the replacement of public housing with condos.

Reporter Naomi Klein, while standing in line for food in a shelter, overheard an exhausted inner city resident respond, What is wrong with these people in Baton Rouge? This isn't an opportunity. It's a goddamned tragedy. Are they blind? A mother with two kids chimed in, "No, they're not blind, they're evil. They see just fine."[68]

An impossibility to most minds is the potential to actually orchestrate a disaster and then profit from it in some way. So inconceivable is this that most will label it a "conspiracy theory" and walk the other way. Is it possible that events like 9/11, bombings, assassinations, mass shootings, the initiation of wars and even pandemics could have been tacitly allowed or even orchestrated by wolves for some type of consolidation of power or to implement measures that run contrary to deeply held public beliefs? The more intractable the belief, the greater the crisis needed to break down public resistance against that course of action.

---

68. Naomi Klein, *The Shock Doctrine: The Rise of Disaster Capitalism*, (New York, 2007), 4–5.

An attempt to argue the case would go far afield of this book, and there is an abundance of material already in existence (see recommended reading in appendix). Lance DeHaven-Smith, a professor of Public Administration and Policy at Florida State University and author of *Conspiracy Theory in America*, argues that a suspicious attitude toward government is crucial to maintaining our democracy and supported by the realistic view of mankind and the potential for political corruption and misconduct foreseen by The Founders in the Declaration of Independence.

Labeling someone who is suspicious of criminal wrongdoing at the highest levels of government a "conspiracy theorist" effectively frames them as paranoid crazies whose arguments should be rejected out of hand, a convenient way of avoiding rebuttal with evidence—a much better choice if evidence exists.

Non-Event Stagecraft

Non-Event Stagecraft is wholesale fabrication of an event in order to manipulate public opinion. This works most effectively as an offshore tactic where cross-checking and story validation are nearly impossible for the average person due to language and cultural barriers, as well as travel and other costs. The Kuwait Witness is a good example of this category as well as the Gulf of Tonkin incident that propelled the United States into war with North Vietnam.

Restoration of Normalcy

Earlier it was noted that the approach of human beings to unknown territory is deeply embedded. Known territory constitutes order, safety, and security. People exposed to increasingly challenging unknown situations—from novel to disconcerting, threatening, and chaos itself, exhibit a natural inborn impulse to return to the safety and security of known territory.

Humans function poorly in chaotic environments, which is why we create culture and norms that tend to render the world safe and predictable. Loss of this stability creates a community-wide rush to restore order. This has long been known and exploited.

It is epitomized by the Latin phrase *Ordo Ab Chao*—"Order Out of Chaos." Chaos unleashes a primordial force in all living things that yearns for the restoration of normalcy. Those who understand this group dynamic and are willing to exploit it know that many will seize upon the first offer of order regardless of the wisdom of the decision. This can and often does result in catastrophic loss of hard-won freedoms in exchange for safety and security—an incredibly bad bargain in the long run.

This has also been described as "Problem, Reaction, Solution." Staged events create a problem which leads to a reaction and the demand for a solution which has already been predetermined, waiting in the wings to be implemented.

It's brilliant, of course. And the edifice upon which to easily conceal this malevolent operation—the unwarranted naivety of the public: "They would NEVER do this in a democracy." "They," meaning the wolves in corporations, branches of the military, government officials and influential bankers. The simulation of democracy, think Wizard of Oz, is the curtain behind which the wolf pack does their work.

Operation Sheepskin is consent manufacturing on steroids. In the next chapter, you'll be shown how it's possible to go beyond the successful implementation of problem-reaction-solution to literally create a false reality and not just a narrative by vamping or hijacking trust throughout societal institutions, thus forming Operation Spider's Web.

DOES EVIL EXIST?

Contemplating the magnitude of evil required to engage in such subversive, corrupt and treasonous actions is difficult. To most people, evil belongs to a realm somewhere remote and far away, relegated to the dark ages. Most of modern society views God as dead along with the evil force that opposed Him. After all, where are the screaming Hitlers and the stacks of dead bodies? Could evil perhaps be hiding behind silk Armani suits in comfortable board rooms across America?

The illusion of the United States as having retained superior moral high ground throughout the twentieth century is quite strong as it is fed and maintained by our very own educational system.

It would be naïve to believe that the most powerful and prosperous country in the world would be immune from the infiltration of those with evil intents and motivations. As Weaver notes, "those who say that evil is but a bad dream or an accident of history or the creation of a few antisocial men are only preparing us for worse disillusionments and disasters."[69]

The honest way to approach this knowledge gap is to examine the counterarguments made by those who are whistleblowers, truth seekers mining declassified government documents, historical researchers and alternative news reporters. Refute them if you can. We'll look more into this in coming chapters.

Bernays masterfully prototyped the novel stagecraft approach and, in return, was paid handsomely by the corporations. It was nearly impossible for hard-working and otherwise preoccupied citizens to detect this subversion of the news. They trusted what they saw on television and believed reports about those events in good faith.

---

69. Ted Smith, ed., *In Defense of Tradition: Collected Shorter Writings of Richard Weaver*, 1929–1963, (Indiana, 2000), 45.

Does it seem plausible that those with almost unlimited finances having witnessed the success and vast potential of the ring of power . . . the power to compel behavior, the power to transform society without force, the power to consolidate financial resources would have abandoned it for the good of the nation?

Let's not let wishful thinking and/or willful blindness shield us from the ugly truth of what is staring us right in the face.

SUMMARY

What makes Operation Sheepskin so dangerous is its conversion from a lone wolf use of propaganda to a pack of wolves preying on the underclass through its ability to manipulate the masses. The techniques of propaganda are consolidated between separate sources of power working in concert. It is organized crime using propaganda in coordinated and systematic campaigns. They outline the goals and lay out the events needed to steer the public into directions that produce piles of cash and control for themselves, their friends and allies.

Operation Sheepskin absolutely depends on the media acting as the tribal elders to lead the public through the problem-reaction-solution framework that creates a cover story for the desired hidden agenda.

The inherent response of primal brain architecture to unknown territory is the reason why collective experiences out of the ordinary are the most powerful tool in the wolves' arsenal for shifting behaviors and beliefs. The sheep desire to be led to safety and security.

People "witness or experience" an event—which could be a non-event, a real event with a false interpretation, or staged events along a continuum from interesting to threatening. The problem to be solved is magnified across media channels. The reaction to the problem is carefully documented. Something must be done. Cue up the alternatives. Lead the sheep to the correct solution.

Once you learn to recognize the obvious patterns, it becomes child's play to understand much of the confusing optics of democratic politics. Reverse engineering the proposal of new laws, policy, and "wars" will now be easier than you ever imagined. You have the power.

In the next chapter, we will learn how the techniques used by the organized crime network in Operation Sheepskin can be broadened to create Operation Spider's Web, a surround sound of authoritative voices in the culture and an ideological scaffolding so pervasive that it constitutes a pseudo-reality.

Let's find out what the wolves are up to.

Chapter 8
OPERATION SPIDER'S WEB

Mark Twain once said, "It is easier to fool people than it is to convince them that they have been fooled." Arguably it is better to avoid being fooled in the first place than attempt to undo the damage after the fact, and this is, of course, why you are reading this book.

If you have ever been made to play the fool, you know how humiliating it is to reveal the circumstances. For some strange reason, it is almost second nature to believe it is easy to detect a fraud or a con artist as if we had been born with some type of innate warning device. Unfortunately, new fools are minted every day. Why are we so blind to our vulnerability and so cocksure of our infallibility?

It all centers around the difference between earned trust and implicit trust. No one will be fooled if a stranger walks into a room and tries to sell them land in Florida. There is no reason to trust him. He emerged literally out of nowhere. Trust on a local level is earned before being granted. One hundred years ago, when small local communities thrived, neighbors who were well acquainted knew who was trustworthy and who was not.

Con artists know that building trust takes time because character is only revealed through action. Instead, they prefer to use shortcuts like charm, flattery, winsome behavior, and alluring promises to gain trust. A smiling face conceals the true risk. Once trust is established, victims lower their guard, assuming danger has passed. Should their true character be revealed, they disappear. Exposed for selling "snake oil?" Head off to a new town or new victim; start over with fresh faces and a sterling new reputation to sow beguiling seeds once more.

The propagandist, a close cousin to the con artist, uses those same methods to establish trust and lure their victims into the net. Trust is the vital relational substrate they crave.

Similarly, local politicians are shipwrecked if exposed as liars. Proximity to leadership in tight-knit communities made ongoing deception tricky, thus safeguarding the community against the con man and his arts.

On the other hand, distance facilitated the con artist's maneuvers and made communities more vulnerable over time. National leadership packaged and sold through the media, with all its warts removed, has grown increasingly unaccountable. Lacking close personal contact or community interaction, identifying and weeding out the untrustworthy becomes untenable. Leadership remains veiled and distant; attempts to match words with deeds—vital to assessing character—a real nightmare.

But of course, this is what the news media is for, right? Independent from government and committed to revealing the truth about current events, the press lives and breathes for the express purpose of exposing frauds and liars.

As I have repeatedly attempted to show, the news media is unfortunately no longer the watchdog of the state apparatus but an ally. Independent media, driven by citizen journalists, are working to fill in the gaps, but lack of critical manpower, resources, and finances makes the job an uphill battle.

Failure of the mainstream media to vet hucksters, frauds, liars, and cheats creates a gash in the wall of protection around the society. Great as that injury may be, it is minuscule compared with the damage inflicted by weaponization of the press on behalf of hostile interests. Incompetence is one thing, treachery another.

As bad a turn of events as this is for the people who need information to navigate a complex world and are forced to rely on unvetted authorities, please remember that the propagandist has his share of problems as well. Human trustworthiness is fragile and easily exhausted. When deeds finally catch up to words and flimsy promises, another freshly minted personality vetted for allegiance to outside interests must be positioned to move up the ranks to supplant worn-out politicians whose public reputations are tarnished beyond repair.

Propagandists, just like con artists, are the equivalent of "trust vampires"—constantly requiring new victims from which to "vamp" trust. Without trust, the lies and deceptions fail. Relying on human capital alone to hoodwink the masses is problematic.

The good news for the propagandist is that individuals aren't the only ones to accumulate trust. Professions accumulate trust, as well as nonprofit organizations, non-governmental organizations, foundations, institutions, think tanks, celebrities, educational institutions and, of course, science.

What if propagandists could hijack that trust?

What if they could promote their own agenda while siphoning trust from many other places?

What if they could even co-opt respected organizations by capturing a few key leadership positions and then push their agenda through that organization?

What if they had plenty of money with which to buy off

or blackmail respected leaders? The fact is: Yes, they can, and yes, they do. Welcome to "Operation Spider's Web."

Operation Sheepskin is an extraordinary tool for manipulating public opinion on selected issues and consolidating power. Any singular campaign can draw influence from authorities, but what I am suggesting now is a much broader and wide sweeping use of the pillar of Authority. Can you sense the potential for maximal reorganization of society?

Quite simply, vamping trust from a coalition of respected entities converts Operation Sheepskin into Operation Spider's Web by multiplying its force and effectiveness exponentially.

Altering public perceptions on issues is almost rudimentary compared to the incredible ability to create—planetary realities.

As was noted in Chapter 4, propaganda is a rich man's sport. Imagine with piles of money you can purchase "trust," enabling you to monopolize ideas. Your ideas at the top of the food chain ensure continued market dominance and financial leverage over a manipulated citizenry. You are going to do this in various ways; creating foundations that will "donate" large sums of money to organizations you would like to influence, sponsoring organizations that influence national and global leaders and by creating nonprofit organizations that can promote your message while appearing independent.

This takes decades, but you're a patient person. After all, global ideological dominance shouldn't happen overnight. When sufficient entities exist or have been captured—the average citizen is subject to the finest pseudo-reality that money can buy. It's a diabolical achievement—the corruption and take-over of the ideological free market. Your ideas saturate the landscape, and your helpless victims struggle to triangulate "truth," trapped in a literal spider's web of interconnected and well-financed authoritative voices and entities.

Fiction, you say?

SPIDER'S WEB OF POWER

C. Wright Mills, a sociologist (1956), writing in *The Power Elite*, classified this group as "those in command of the major hierarchies and organizations of modern society. They rule the big corporations. They run the machinery of the state and claim its prerogatives. They direct the military establishment. They occupy the strategic command posts of the social structure." He concluded that it was the power elite who decided whatever is decided of major consequence. The fact that this book remains in print sixty years after it was written is evidence of the staying power of his critique.

If we jump to the future, we see a similar understanding being offered by yet another sociologist Peter Phillips from Sonoma State University, in his book *Giants: The Global Power Elite* (2017). During Mill's time, the power elite was able to exert dominance over a singular nation-state, but this restriction has been erased, and a new term in academia has emerged, "The Transnational Capitalist Class" or TCC. They are one percent of the world's wealthiest people who provide the ideological justification driving desired actions to be implemented worldwide in pursuit of their shared interests through transnational governmental organizations. What? That sounds like conspiracy theory! But wait . . . this is current academic nomenclature.

Phillips uncovers the vast web of interconnectedness of the seventeen giant investment firms managing in excess of 43 trillion dollars in capital, who are themselves cross-invested with each other, the near giants (close to 1 trillion dollar portfolios), and have ownership stakes in the top fifteen hundred corporations spanning the globe giving them enormous power in corporate board rooms across the planet. Leaders of these firms meet together at various policy-making conferences throughout the year to network, strategize and finalize recommendations in the form of reports and whitepapers that heavily influence worldwide geopolitics.

In a chapter entitled, *Ideologists; Corporate Media and Public Relation Propaganda Firms – Selling Empire, War and Capitalism*, Phillips examines the corporate media and what he calls Public Relation Propaganda firms (PRPs) which astonishingly are controlled and dominated by the very same monied interests as the corporations. Phillips estimates that two-thirds to 80 percent of corporate media's content from broadcast and print news come directly from public relations and propaganda firms, meaning "nearly all content inside the global corporate media system today is pre-packaged, managed news, opinion, and entertainment."[70]

The three largest public relations propaganda firms (PRPs), WPP, Omnicom Group and the Interpublic Group, are deeply interlocked with the corporate media, the military-industrial complex, and the policy elites. New York City-based Omnicom alone boasted an annual revenue of $15.2 billion in 2017, managing 74,000 employees in more than 200 agencies represented by subsidiaries, affiliates, and quasi-independent agencies such as BBDO worldwide, DDB Worldwide and many others. Omnicom's major clients include more than 5,000 brands, universities, nonprofits and NGOs (Non-Governmental Organizations).

The London-based WPP had an annual revenue of $21.1 billion as of 2017, with around 190,000 employees working across 112 countries. Some noteworthy clients of WPP are Amazon, Microsoft, NBC, Healthline, Golden Globes and the Grammy Awards, as well as The World Economic Forum, The NFL and Pfizer. Interpublic Group's clientele is similarly diverse, including the US Army, California State Lottery, ABC, Columbia Records, Unilever, US Bank, Facebook, and ExxonMobil—just to name a few.

70. Phillips, 263.

From 2007 to 2015, the federal government of the United States spent more than 4 billion on public relations services, employing 3,092 public relations officers, not to mention an additional 2.2 billion paid to outside firms like Young & Rubicam, Ogilvy Public Relations Worldwide, Burson-Marsteller and Laughlin, Marinaccio & Owens for polling, research, and market consulting who collectively pocketed tens of millions of dollars of taxpayer money in 2014.

In contrast to their high-profile companies and clients with powerful name recognition, the names of elite PR firms are relatively unknown and obscure sounding forgettable versions of Acme, Inc. Obviously, the branding experts do not themselves wish to be known to the population at large, but Wall Street knows who they are. The total annual investment in Omnicom Group alone by the financial giants? $4.06 billion, including Blackrock ($1.25 billion), Vanguard Group ($1.24 billion), State Street ($699 million) and ten more—you get the point.

If you still live in the dark ages thinking there is no intertwined global elite controlling and overpowering the sovereignty of nation-states and dominating the ideological landscape, take the time and read Phillip's book. It's a reality check as bracing as a cold shower. You'll never see the world quite the same again. Philips profiles three hundred eighty-nine of the world's most powerful players in capitalism, their net worth, prior and current employment, board of directors' appointments and their education. It's a very small ecosystem of entwined connections, financial overlap, elite prestige and message control which they inhabit.

A SPIDER'S WEB NEEDS A WEAVER

Does this seem as complex as the intricacy of a Spider's Web? There are integrations, cross integrations, partnerships, overlap of leadership and constant networking among the one percent.

This is evident. So far, an obvious but overlooked question is: If a deeply complex geo-political and ideological web has already been established, who are the weavers and what are they up to? Who is responsible for the organization on such a grand scale?

People who study these types of things have many names for the weavers: "The Deep State," "The One Percent," "The Elites," "GloboCap," "The Powers That Be," or simply "Globalists." It is likely that the true leaders will always remain hidden, and the leaders profiled in Phillips' book are more or less figureheads fronting for controllers behind the scenes. Remember, wolves don't go announcing themselves to the general public. If things go awry, their anonymity protects them. In the end, knowledge of the names is not as important as understanding the systematic game of winner take all that they are playing.

For the purposes of this book, the important point to remember is that the weavers are already well past subverting the governance of the United States and have moved on to the task of global control.

For a basic knowledge of that subversion, I'd like to recommend *The Rockefeller Files* and *None Dare Call It Conspiracy* by Gary Allen as a great starting point because he tracks and follows the big foundation money in politics early mid-century through the eighties. Another good read is *Conspirators' Hierarchy: The Story of the Committee of 300* by Dr. John Coleman, and finally, for the stout of heart, you can tackle *The Anglo-American Establishment* and/or *Tragedy and Hope* by Carroll Quigley.

My primary purpose is to map out how that leadership group, whoever they are, has successfully manipulated public opinion to serve interests that are at odds with the American people—without their knowledge.

Let's return to that quest by examining how the elite are able to create a virtual pseudo-reality by establishing an intellectual cartel that maintains a chokehold on the perennial idea incubators in society—the universities and the men who walk those halls.

FOUNDATIONS – ORGANIZED CHARITY TO CHLOROFORM PUBLIC OPINION?

Encyclopedia Britannica editors called WWI with its censorship, war bias and "perversion of fact" a grand canyon gash in the whole intellectual structure of the world."[71]

What arose to fill that void? The philanthropic foundation. The outspoken George Creel (future head of the Committee on Public Information), in response to news that the Rockefeller Foundation was conducting a million-dollar investigation into the cause of industrial unrest provoked by the miner's strike in Colorado, queried, "Is organized charity no more than a carefully premeditated fraud, designed by unscrupulous millionaires to chloroform public opinion and nothing more than a scheme to muddy the waters?"[72]

It's ironic, given Creel's role in WWI propaganda, that he prophetically saw the rise of toxic charity: the giving of money that functions more like a dreaded poison ruining the health of the intellectual marketplace than a welcomed elixir fostering clarity, innovation and common-sense wisdom to the body politic.

The Reese Committee warning that the rise and growth of charitable foundations "may someday control our whole intellectual and cultural life—and with it the future of this country" was not mere hyperbole. The committee's investigation was replete with documents and testimony proving that "this intellectual cartel has already been felt deeply in education and in the political scene."[73]

---

71. John Maxwell Hamilton, *Manipulating The Masses: Woodrow Wilson and the Birth of American Propaganda*, (Baton Rouge, 2020), 454.
72. Auerbach, 62.
73. Rene A Wormser, *Foundations: Their Power and Influence*, (New York, 1958), 68.

The first investigation into foundation work, nicknamed the Cox Committee, was brought into existence by the 83rd Congress to examine the affairs of tax-exempt foundations to determine if resources were being used for the purposes for which they were established and if those same foundations were using their resources for un-American or subversive activities not in the interest or tradition of the United States.

Given the numerous friends the giant foundations had secured over previous decades, the investigation amounted to little more than a glorified press conference highlighting their extensive contributions to society. Not surprisingly, the committee ruled that there was little basis for concern about foundation funds being diverted from their intended use.

Representative Reese from TN was not so easily dissuaded and sensing that there was more under the carpet than had yet to be uncovered. He lobbied fervently for a much more comprehensive investigation to be launched in the 84th Congress and was granted his wish.

The Committee was hobbled from the start; fearing the viability of the committee itself, it was forced to barter away two of its ableist research assistants in exchange for maintaining a mere half of its original appropriations. They forged ahead despite delays and denials of access to critical information, a relentless barrage of criticism from the media, and a myriad of sustained attacks from a minority member of the committee, Rep Hayes from Ohio, a partisan hack intent on sabotaging the inner workings of the committee and the hearings.

Ultimately, the committee was forced to end hearings early and publish what reports it could from the fiasco. The result: Few if any of their warnings about the concentration of power and influence wielded by the foundations across academia, education and international affairs reached the public.

You can read about Rep Hayes' chronic, rude and unstatesmanlike behavior in Rene Wormser's *Foundations: Their*

Power and Influence, where this man's churlish behavior is now immortalized.

Why the urgent need to shipwreck the investigation? What might the wolves be hiding? Is it really possible to create an intellectual cartel, marginalize the innovative men that seed new and creative ideas and monopolize the realm of ideas itself?

An idea syndicate can exist only by capturing the influencers of society—a formidable task. Influencers are, by nature, leaders among men and not easily tethered or shackled to the whims of other men, regardless of the money or prestige offered to them. It is much easy to create a generation of "pseudo-influencers" who willingly prostrate themselves to the bidding of others through the lure of grants and the promise of appointments, publications, and prestige. While elevating the less worthy, the same system throttles men of high intelligence and independent spirits. This is exactly what happened to Professors Hobbs, a sociologist and one of the men that testified before the Reese Committee.

His supervisor at the University of Pennsylvania had told him in no uncertain terms that he had no hope of rising in the hierarchy because he was a known dissident and critic of the methods used in the foundation-supported complex of research in social science and, therefore, he jokingly called himself the "oldest assistant professor east of the Rockies."

Wormser described him like this . . .

He is brilliant and exceptionally well informed. He is given to independent thought, a precious commodity in our society. But he pays the price of independence. He supports his family on the salary of a laborer. He stands as one of the object-lessons to academicians: Conform or Be Damned."[74]

In contrast, Professor Harold Lasswell, a contemporary of Hobbs, was one of the academics upon whom foundation

74. Ibid, 88–89

patronage had been bestowed lavishly. "He was one of the influential 'experts' in the social sciences on whom foundation managers have so often relied for the selection of projects and the allocation of funds."[75] His position with the foundations led to his being elected president of the American Political Science Association.

I quoted Lasswell, the author of *Propaganda Technique in the World War* (1927), in an earlier chapter. He stands as an example of the type of man sought out and elevated by the Foundations to stature beyond the measure of his character. The darling of foundation money gave us this ominous prophesy—a gem that is as astonishing in its arrogance as in its condescension:

> *Propaganda is a concession to the willfulness of the age. The bonds of personal loyalty and affection which bound a man to his chief have long since dissolved. Monarchy and class privilege have gone the way of all flesh, and the idolatry of the individual passes for the official religion of democracy. It is an atomized world, in which individual whims have wider play than ever before, and it requires more strenuous exertions to co-ordinate and unify than formerly. The new antidote to willfulness is propaganda. If the mass will be free of chains of iron, it must accept its chains of silver. If it will not love, honor and obey, it must not expect to escape seduction.*[76]

Make no mistake, that was directed at you—the reader. Lasswell is the prototypical man foundation money hath wrought.

The second way in which to create an idea syndicate is to control the realm of ideas by lavishly funding certain themes and narratives while selectively starving others slated for extinction. The true threat of the foundations lies "in their ability to provide

75. Ibid, 53.
76. Harold D. Lasswell, *Propaganda Technique in The World War*, (New York, 1938), 222.

war chests in the battle of ideas," picking winners and losers and corrupting the free-flowing ideological landscape.[77]

During the depression, private universities and colleges were squeezed for income, presidents of those institutions could not readily afford to ignore or turn down sizable foundation grants even if such money was earmarked for projects inconsistent with their policy, priority of goals or urgent needs because displeasing foundation executives might mean being overlooked in the next round of largess.

The following schematic is how the Reece Committee conceptualized the broad sweeping interlock of foundation influence operating as a quasi-monopoly in education, the social science, and international affairs.

IDEA SYNDICATE

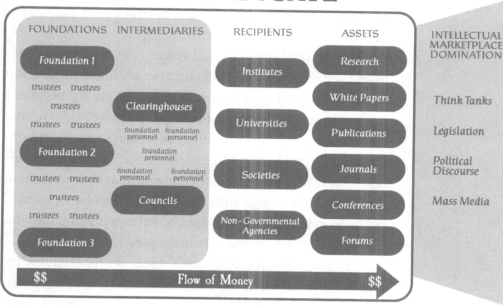

The true threat of the foundations lies "in their ability to provide war chests in the battle of ideas," picking winners and losers and corrupting the free-flowing ideological landscape.

77. Wormser, 40.

The intermediaries are jointly created by several foundations and function as centralized coordinating agencies that operate as instruments of control by claiming supreme authority in a field despite being staffed in many cases without representation by rank and file experts in the field.

Money is rarely distributed without strings. The foundations favor their own pet projects, programs, and personnel in addition to supplying detailed operational budgets to the extent that, in some cases, the only thing supplied by the participating institution is their name and prestige, functioning more like a department of the foundation than a separate entity.

Grants were given to certain select universities more frequently than others leading to even further consolidation of intellectual capital. Columbia, The University of Chicago, Stanford University, and The University of North Carolina were several of the highly funded institutions at the time of the Reece Committee.

The demand for empirical research as evidence of academic achievement eventually became another control point of the foundation gravy train. "Publish or perish" became a precondition for advancement on the academic ladder of success. Research requires funding, and professors wanting to move up the ladder would need to toe the line of idea orthodoxy. Those ideas that are nonconformist, unconventional or simply do not comport with the dominant ideology espoused by the foundation trustees would be left to wither on the vine, having little reach or power to influence.

Much of what is called "truth" today is supported by "research." The "research" says . . . is the essence of supposed objectivity and the backbone of a superior argument leaving the fellow without research in the dust. The logic is as follows: All worthy ideas get funding for research; your ideas have no supporting research; therefore, your ideas are inferior.

As you can easily see, all ideas do not have equal opportunity to advance if the control lever of funding is biased. With this scheme in place, entire intellectual flotillas of specialized science could be created and used to commandeer social policy, legislation, and judicial rulings by directing the money spigots flowing into academia.

The Reece committee was able to ascertain the dangers stemming from a virtual idea syndicate. Their tragically muted warning cries out to us today from the dustbins of history. The Foundation's chokehold on the marketplace of ideas has remained hidden and unchallenged; they alone will give birth to the ideas Americans embrace; the grant-writing "losers" can lick their wounds and go home.

Foundation control of monies to academia can be thought of as a chokehold on the seedbed or ideological germination centers targeting idea creators and their livelihood. In this next section, I'll describe the use of front groups as a means to influence or capture the flow of ideas targeted directly at Joe consumer or Joe citizen.

FRONT GROUPS

A Front Group is the all-purpose con, a way to sell to the sheep by stealth what wolves themselves cannot through the "neutral" front of a third-party organization. "Neutral" organizations are created and/or funded by corporations, government, or organizations for a particular tactical purpose. Funding sources are hidden or only selectively disclosed in order to be perceived by the public as unbiased and to hide the real agenda, which is solely economic or strategic in nature.

As public-interest lawyer Michele Simon writes in *The Best Public Relation Money Can Buy:*

> *Front groups often have deceptive sounding names and attempt to create a positive public impression that hides*

their funder's economic motives. Through running media campaigns, providing friendly and accessible spokespeople to the media, producing reports, and even supplying curricula to public schools, front groups have proven to be an effective strategy in shaping public opinion and fighting unfavorable policy.[78]

Remember, the funding required to create and sustain organizations for fraudulent purposes is beyond the reach of most people.

All of the following conglomerates routinely use front groups to promote their agenda, including "Big Pharma," "Big Agriculture," "Big Education," "Big Medicine," and "Big Environment."

The use of third-party technique or front groups by public relations experts has been around since the infancy of the profession. Back in the early 1900s, Stannard Baker uncovered "anti-trucker" front groups sponsored and funded by the railroad to discourage competition from the trucking industry.

In fact, there were two noteworthy anti-trust lawsuits based on the Sherman Act, The A&P Chain Store litigation in 1945 and the battle of the Southern railroad versus the Pennsylvania truckers in 1953, that touched on the ethics and legality of the technique.

In the courtroom, lawyers argued that their use enabled powerful agents in their quest to maintain or create monopolies. In the end, the courts punted away the opportunity to safeguard the public by ruling that because the technique could be used by either side, irrespective of its deceptive tactics, it should be allowed to influence public opinion, thereby

78. Hamerschlag, Lappe, and Malkan, *The Friends of Earth, Spinning Food: How Food Industry Front Groups and Covert Communications Are Shaping the Story of Food.* PDF online (2015), 10.

cementing as commonplace the contamination of the ideological marketplace in favor of those with the money.[79]

Unlikely Origin of An "American" Front Group

Least you think that industries are the only guilty parties using front groups; the following story is a prime example of how this tactic was used by Great Britain in WWII as seen through the eyes of George Eggleston, an editor of Life Magazine with a front row seat to the controversies of the time.

In the late thirties, Col. Charles Lindbergh and others who saw war clouds gathering in Europe were determined to prevent America's entry into the second world war. Eggleston agreed that a second "War-to-end War" was to be opposed and, as a result, changed jobs accepting a leading position with *Scribner's Commentator*, a new magazine whose sole purpose was dedicated to keeping America out of World War II. At the time, eighty percent of Americans opposed entering the war, and the "America First" movement was strong and flourishing.

As the Lend-Lease Act was winding its way through congress, legislation crafted to push the very limits of assistance to the allies while still maintaining a veneer of neutrality, a new "pro-war" group sprang up seemingly out of nowhere, the Fight for Freedom Committee. Their pamphlets denounced Lindbergh and other senators and congressmen as appeasers, engaged in wild claims that the Germans had massacred 1,500,000 men and women in Poland and constantly harped on the theme that the fall of Western Civilization was at hand unless the barbaric Germans were crushed.

The source of the group remained a mystery to Eggleston for years until he read *A Man Called Intrepid* by William Stevenson. Eggleston stumbled upon the revelation some thirty

---

79. Cutlip, 570-581.

years after the war had ended as he was preparing to write *Roosevelt, Churchill and the World War II Opposition: A Revisionist Autobiography,* his personal account of the harassment suffered at the hands of the Roosevelt administration for opposing America's entry into World War II.

Intrepid was the code name for William Stephenson, the chief of all British Intelligence Services worldwide. He commanded over 30,000 intelligence personnel scattered across the globe and another 2,000 specialists under his supervision while operating out of two floors of the Rockefeller Center in New York City.

Intrepid was Winston Churchill's undercover representative assigned to make sure FDR brought America into the war. In his book, Intrepid proudly takes credit for creating and directing the "Fight for Freedom Committee" and supplying them with money and false information.

As Eggleston and others were getting harassed by the IRS, accused of being financed by the Germans, they came up with an idea to not only exonerate themselves but to expose the finances of the Fight for Freedom Committee. They called for a senate investigation into the activities of any person, committee or corporation acting for or on behalf of any foreign nation for propaganda purposes, including themselves. The investigation never materialized, and the truth remained hidden for over 30 years—Great Britain had been funding a multimillion-dollar propaganda operation on U.S. soil a full two years before the United States' entry into the war. The Fight for Freedom Committee, a British front group, used enormous resources to market yet another war to the American people.

With enough money, front groups can afford to scheme up designer truth hot off the assembly line to support literally any platform. As investigative journalist Cynthia Crossen explains in *Tainted Truth: The Manipulation of Fact in America,* findings from surveys and polls can be manipulated countless ways through design tweaks to increase the probability of churning out "truth" to support almost any agenda.

Thanks to billions of dollars spent through foundations, public relations firms and the third-party technique, Americans are literally swimming in a sea of manufactured truth, ubiquitous and ever-present. The proliferation of manufactured "authorities" for the promotion of ideas at arm's length from the true authors are designed to ensure your receptivity and disable your native instincts to smell a stinker when you encounter one.

I hope by now you are already beginning to visualize the outline of the Spider's Web.

OPERATION SPIDER'S WEB

Operation Spider's Web is essentially the monopolization of ideas and the capture of leadership in the learned professions and important societal institutions. The tribal elders of the news are still doing their thing, identifying problems, narrating stories and interpreting events for the masses as described in Operation Sheepskin. But now, they are surrounded by and supported at every turn in the road by idea orthodoxy and by captured authorities that guide and shape community opinions. As idea orthodoxy metastasizes throughout the system, social pressure to conform is intensified dramatically, leading to what some people are prone to call mass psychosis. After all, "everyone who is anyone" believes the main storyline. You must be a loon if you think otherwise.

One pillar of *The Infrastructure of Belief,* Authority, multiplied by the power of eight different sectors of society, forming a sticky mental web of group think nearly impossible to escape unless one has been trained to recognize patterns.

As we already know, people inherently seek out, consult, and triangulate authoritative sources in a community when confronted with confusing or conflicting information or stories. They look to professionals like doctors, lawyers, and professors, respected nonprofit organizations, think tanks, trusted politicians, legal rulings, science, and even celebrities to navigate and ascertain truth. This was true in Le Bon's time, and it's even more relevant today. Through technology, the reliance on nonlocal sources for truth dramatically increases vulnerability to propaganda.

These sources do more than just enhance and reinforce the media narrative and/or supply solutions to the questions raised in Operation Sheepskin; they function as a sclerotic, mentally rigid framework of the world, a surround sound of pseudo-reality which permeates the populace and strangles the vibrant idea ecology that it has replaced.

Going back to the idea of mass formation psychosis, this is simply social pressure/contagion writ large, the natural progression of authority corruption. When a majority of the people believe a certain way, it is always difficult to go against the grain.

Attempting to communicate with people who completely reject an honest appraisal of alternative narratives feels like one is communicating with those who've been brainwashed or are in some type of trance, but the web of authorities spouting the party line is so vast and systemic that their triangulation system simply locks onto that "trust" and dismisses other non-authoritative sources as garbage. To a person who has paid scant attention to history or devoted minimal mental energy to see past the curtain of propaganda, a suggestion that multiple authoritative sources of trust in society have been corrupted seemingly all at once in their uncritical minds is preposterous. They dwell peacefully in the safe and secure pseudo-reality they have accepted unquestioningly.

The appeal to "Trust science" as an "uncorrupted" and "pristine" body of knowledge that can be relied upon in times of confusion even when politicians are viewed as untrust-worthy and unreliable is an example of how institutional trust can be vamped for ulterior motives.

Understanding this type of brain lock from the *Infrastructure of Belief* model forces us to look critically at the systems that give rise to authorities in this brave new world of ours and the vast subterranean pool of corruption existing below the surface of our consciousness. Mislabeling the phenomenon mass formation or a type of hypnosis makes it likely that we miss the deeper work needed for the transformation of a terminally sick society.

Adoption of a mass formation model has us searching for . . . the voodoo doll with pins to undo the hypnotic spell. Where exactly does society go with this conceptualization? It simply obscures from our vision the reality of systemic corruption in the ideological marketplace and in the selection of weak, compromised leaders who will espouse any idea so long as they themselves are enriched financially and growing in power and prestige.

For those locked in the trance, I believe the answer is to see historically how pervasively and methodically the system has been corrupted over the past century. Arguments that remain rooted in contemporary events are unlikely to sway the brain-locked sheep one wit from their trust in authorities. It is easier for them to believe that the carrier of a competing narrative is a Martian from planet Zenon, even if it's their very own spouse than it is to have their entire framework of trust demolished in one sitting. It's a psychological shock and a blow to the ego that they will ward off with a vengeance.

TOTAL BLOCKADE

To fully establish Operation Spider's Web, competing views must be tightly controlled. Alternative explanations punch holes in the created pseudo-reality, like air being let out of a balloon.

The move to create and sustain Operation Spider's Web across an entire culture is much more tenuous than establishing a single narrative or campaign like Operation Sheepskin. It demands greater vigilance in the suppression of ideas and ultimately the silencing of people who refuse to accept the agreed-upon narrative.

This suppression must be swift and thorough so that the narrative has time to harden into orthodoxy without being adequately questioned. As Orwell explains below, an orthodoxy is simply a body of ideas that is mindlessly assumed to be correct by all "right-thinking" people. The time for analysis is considered to be already past.

In Appendix A, there is a list of the myriad ways in which the media control and/or suppress ideas that are competing with the dominant narrative. Also noted are ways to control and censor people who hold unorthodox ideas damaging to the preferred narrative.

Of course, the media must make sure other narratives receive airtime to maintain the illusion of neutrality and unbiased reporting, with one exception; truth that has the power to unseat the illusion of democracy will have a firewall erected against it to prevent its emergence into the free market of ideas. The firewall is a complete barrier to the mainstream media.

After Mark Lane, a respected trial lawyer, wrote his first book on the Kennedy assassination, *Rush to Judgment*, there was a total media blockade to prevent its publication and distribution in the United States.

The blackout of coverage on potential election fraud in the 2020 campaign is another example of wall-to-wall censorship critical to maintaining the illusion of democracy. Why the media blackout if you can easily refute the allegations and prove them false for all to see? Isn't that the better alternative?

The recent documentary *2000 Mules* demonstrates clear voter fraud with indisputable video footage. The extent of the fraud amounted to hundreds of thousands of write-in ballots being cast in multiple swing states via mules, a term to describe individuals identified by cell locator systems to have made multiple visits not only to certain ballot boxes but also to nearby nonprofits identified as the source of the extra ballots. Clearly, there was fraud associated with the write-in ballots. Most of the media has mentioned this documentary only for the purpose of debunking it.

Dissenting opinions that are the most compelling and threatening to the system are isolated from the population so as not to be allowed to take root. Stigmatizing nonconformists and free thinkers with derogatory labels seals the operation to cage truth. The sooner a story is settled, the easier it is to tar or feather the dissenters. It sets up a circular argument, "Of course, this is the true story because, well—everyone believes this is the true story.

THE ECOSYSTEM OF IDEAS: FREE SPEECH ZONE

Individuals do not need to be "protected" from ideas. Protection from ideas is a way to disable and cripple free people. The First Amendment to the Constitution ensures that nothing can stand in the way of free speech and a robust marketplace of ideas, whether they be good, bad, or ugly. Of course, therein lies the problem. Labeling and censoring ideas as "good" or "bad," "harmful," or "offensive" ultimately leads to control of ideas in general and cannot be done without suppressing everyone's right to free speech. It's either all or none.

Ideas that are embraced by the culture and that serve as self-defining are not easily dislodged and take outside force and leverage to overcome. A culture has its own inherent values embraced by the majority, who naturally resist values or ideas that undermine their own. In other words, cultures have their own way of "policing" ideas such that dearly held values remain so for years or even decades.

Ideas that are anathema to a strong and vibrant culture, like communism in America during the mid-90s, for example, will be self-censored unless they are being seeded into a culture subversively by sources like the media or educational complex.

Policing ideas or imposing censorship are synthetic ways to resist the organic nature of cultural renewal and to suppress by force the dominant culture seeking to reassert itself. Ideas percolating up from the marketplace are a constant source of refreshing to cultural ideologies that have become stale and unworkable. These organic ideas are authentic ways to challenge the culture vying for hearts and minds through influence and leadership rather than the brute force of censorship.

THE MODEL

Now let's take a more detailed look at a conceptual model of Operation Spider's Web. The center is comprised of the Tribal Elder complex and is surrounded by eight societal institutions endowed with trusted authority used to create, enhance, and sustain the pseudo-reality of Operation Spider's Web. There are eight major sources from which propagandists can vamp or hijack trust:

1. Universities
2. Corporations
3. Medicine
4. Politicians
5. Nonprofit Organizations
6. Justice System
7. Science
8. Government and Regulatory Agencies

OPERATION SPIDER'S WEB
A False Reality

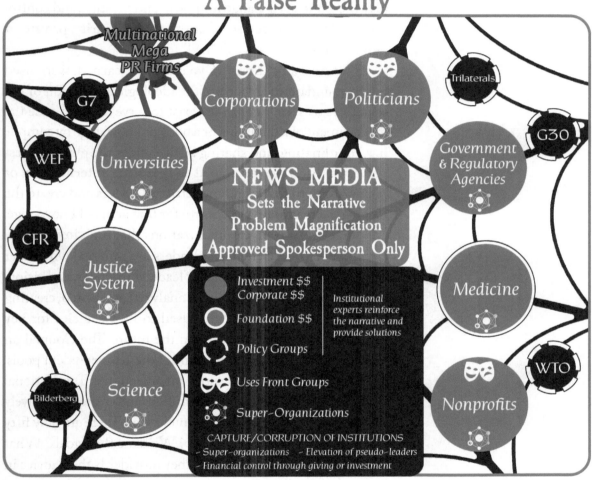

TRIPLE PLAY

At first, it may seem like a difficult thing to take over trusted organizations and/or societal institutions and co-opt their reputation for nefarious ends, but the game plan is really quite simple. There are three important keys: Develop super-organizations, find or promote pseudo-leaders who will play the game in exchange for power and prestige, and control the ideological direction of entities with charity, private or public grants or what I call "bad" money.

Super-organizations, as you already learned, were used by the foundations to control the ideological direction of the social sciences. In theory, they exist to serve and optimize the management of a discipline or a body of knowledge by compiling, coordinating, and sharing advice under the guise of "best practices." They are developed as a network intermediary or policy group to foster and indoctrinate leaders and create the ideological scaffolding of control for that arena of knowledge.

There are also super-organizations that function as leadership pools where emerging leaders are mingled with elder statesmen in forums on topics of leadership, policy, and vision. Young recruits are first critically analyzed and tested, creating a pool of potential applicants used to fill vacancies for key leadership positions that arise in the future. The Council on Foreign Relations functions as one of these super-talent pools.

Another example of a super-organization is The National Governors Association, founded in 1908 and created exclusively for state governors. That's really interesting. There are only fifty governors. Who funds this group? What are their goals? What kind of advice and assistance do they provide? Is their advice in line with the will of the people or in opposition to it?

It turns out there is an abundance of government super-organizations such as the Association of State Health Officials (ASTHO), The Council of State Governments (CSG), the National Association of Counties (NAC), and the National Association of State Treasurers (NAST)—to name just a few.

Remember, you don't have to corrupt vast numbers of individuals or organizations with the media serving as your ally. The media acts as a gatekeeper, highlighting and lauding the corrupt while censoring and belittling honest professionals who will be tempted to retreat from the limelight if their presence creates a firestorm of protest or pushback.

In 2012, Public Citizen, a nonprofit watchdog group, analyzed the sponsorship of many super-organizations like those named above. They concluded that most of the organizations were selling sponsorships to corporations for access to government officials. They reported:

> *There is no doubt that corporate sponsors are getting what they pay for: the ears of decision makers whose decisions will have a direct impact on their bottom lines. Meanwhile, the voices of average citizens are increasingly drowned out, with corporate interests instead of public interest guiding government decisions and actions. These programs overtly undermine the democratic process, allowing corporate interests to have the ear of government officials in a manner that no average citizen can expect to enjoy.*[80]

This is an example of money being used for influence-peddling. Many prominent foundations in America similarly use bad money to steer otherwise well-meaning organizations away from the path of their original charters.

The final piece of this triple play is the power of bad money. The entire mission of organizations can be influenced by money that is given with the intent of controlling and dominating the organization. In other words, it's money with strings attached.

80. https://www.citizen.org/wp-content/uploads/corporate-funding-associations-government-officials.pdf.

SYSTEMIC CORRUPTION

As more and more authoritative sources in the public square are captured, the power to repeat and reinforce the narrative grows exponentially.

The power of Operation Spider's Web has grown and evolved over the past hundred years as more and more social institutions are corrupted, yielding much of their authority to the shady globalists.

Citizens are essentially trapped in a barrage of interlocking and overlapping voices reinforcing the narrative in the service of corrupt leadership—like being caught in a spider's web of disinformation.

Seemingly everywhere, the selected narrative is reinforced by every institution in every facet of society. The populace surrounded by illusory sources of trust hollowed out by corrupted leaders and bad money is isolated and confused adrift in a pseudo-reality more accurately resembling a house of mirrors than real life. The fox has made its way into multiple hen houses of community trust.

Knowledge of the sophistication of early propaganda techniques has been documented so that the reader can readily see the long arc of propagandist history. Without this perspective, it is difficult to fathom the existence of a framework as expansive and diabolical as Operation Spider's Web.

One must acknowledge that a society at this stage is sick and possibly even terminal due to the systemic corruption. Operation Spider's Web is not possible without the wholesale disintegration of much of the leadership's integrity. We are talking about the one to five percent who truly believe they are above the law and the many below them who are willing to compromise their convictions for economic security.

Let's briefly take a look at each of the major sources of trust in a society to highlight areas of corruption or concern. In some cases, I'll direct you to books by whistleblowers where you can gather more information.

Universities

The opinions of professors and university leaders, as well as the research done by institutions, are considered to be trusted sources of truth that can be vamped in support of desired narratives which are then distributed throughout the media.

The massive amounts of money from foundations for building programs, lab construction, and research grants, among other things, have tilted the playing field toward leftist orthodoxy and ideological capture, thoroughly influencing research output and professorial independence. As was demonstrated earlier in the section on Foundations, this has been going on for many years.

Professors who buck the leftist trends are increasingly subject to "cancel culture" and are no longer protected from hostile media attacks. Orthodoxy stifles ideas and is antithetical to the university charter.

Traditionally they have been protected by tenure (a system allowing them to speak freely without fear of losing their job) and a culture that embraced what was once the lifeblood of the university—vibrant idea exchange. Out in the open, ideas can be examined, tested and accepted or rejected, resulting in the constant renewal of society.

Corporations

The multinational brands have clearly given up some measure of independence in exchange for reach and power. How can I say this? Because of their widespread agreement to wade stupidly into toxic social issues that harm rather than enhance their bottom line, far too many well-established brands are rushing headlong over the cliff like a crazed stampede of wildebeests.

Traditionally, corporations steer clear of avant garde social issues, which anger large segments of their customer base if their goal is to make money and maintain the brand loyalty that took them years of painstaking effort and fistfuls of cash to establish.

Social entanglements are anathema for businesses.

Then why are more and more brands entering the political and social fray? What gives?

It's unlikely that CEOs have suddenly become more socially conscious now than in the past. And even if they wanted to be, the financial pressure of shareholders and investors would provide the smelling salts to wake them from their suicidal mission unless the financial stakeholders are themselves sanctioning the suicide missions.

This is, I believe, the only explanation. They are being asked to sacrifice their trust and authority on the altar of the same leftist causes that have dominated academia for the past twenty-five years. Corporations have now joined hands with government and academia to enhance and magnify the echo chamber of "orthodox" causes being pushed mainstream. Open borders, sustainability, climate change, racial and social justice and radical inclusion are the new buzzwords of corporate America.

The majority of these movements or ideologies are not yet mainstream and engender significant social resistance within the culture, especially the support given to the vastly unpopular gender fluidity movement that has been illicitly marketed to children through educational venues.

The cover story is that after 120 years of monopolistic and predatory growth, we are asked to believe that corporations now care about their communities and the people that comprise them.

We are in the midst of a fundamental repositioning of the entire corporate ethos to one of inclusive capitalism which is defined by the Council for Inclusive Capitalism as:

Inclusive capitalism is fundamentally about creating long-term value for all stakeholders—businesses, investors, employees, customers, governments, and communities—guided by an approach that provides: **Equality of opportunity** *for all people to pursue prosperity and quality of life, irrespective of socio-economic background, gender, ethnicity, religion, or age;* **Equitable outcomes** *for those who have the same opportunities and seize them in the same way;* **Fairness across generations** *so that one generation does not realize near-term benefits that incur long-term costs that overburden future generations and* **Fairness in society** *to those whose circumstances prevent them from full economic participation.*[81]

As we shall see later in the chapter, virtually all the major multinational companies are on board with the sustainable development goals created by the United Nations. This transition radically shifts corporate goals from financial to stakeholder-driven—a startling and curious transformation.

It's as if Attila the Hun joined hands with the Pope . . . But wait, did I mention the Pope? That reminds me. The Vatican just joined hands with the Council for Inclusive Capitalism in December 2020. It's being billed as a historic partnership. You can't make this stuff up.

Increasingly, corporations are being asked to function in a surrogate governmental capacity.

The term for this is properly called "corporate fascism."

81. https://www.inclusivecapitalism.com/guiding-principles.

Medicine

There is probably no profession that is held in as high regard as medicine. Physicians have accumulated significant trust with patients over the years. Things are changing, however, as corporations take over hospitals, and doctors have been transformed into mere healthcare providers overburdened with regulations, bureaucratic red tape, heavy debt, and excessive patient loads.

The pharmaceutical industry, by funding everything from journals, conferences, training, and more, has achieved an obscene amount of power over medical protocols. Arguably, drug companies have more and more say in what constitutes standards of care for treatment than doctors do.

I can't think of a better example of Operation Spider's Web leading to an alternative reality than the COVID-19 theater we have all just recently experienced. When I started writing this book in 2018, I could hardly have imagined that a short two years later, the world would fully experience the "megaton power" of Operation Spider's Web to create a fictitious reality that borrows the authority and prestige of science (remember the oft-repeated slogan of "Trust Science") and corrupted super-organizations such as the World Health Organization (WHO), the Centers for Disease Control (CDC), The John Hopkins Institute and The Bill and Melinda Gates Foundation.

Fauci led the campaign, the main goal of which was to create global demand for a vaccine. Of that goal, we may be sure, and the campaign likely has stacked goals, including total surveillance and the Great Reset as promoted by Klaus Schwab and the World Economic Forum (WEF).

Science was corrupted by the inappropriate use of the PCR test as a diagnostic, the promotion of misleading or outright fraudulent research (think NEJM article that was withdrawn at the height of the HQC debate) that was set up to be biased against the benefits of alternative treatments like hydroxychloroquine and ivermectin, and the perverse censorship of doctors advocating their use.

The success and widespread use of either of those drugs to assist COVID-19 patients would have torpedoed the ability of vaccine manufacturers to apply for an Emergency Use Authorization, which is given out only in the absence of viable treatment options!

Politicians

Most politicians have to get approved by the local apparatus of the Republican or Democrat Party and party donors in order to mount a campaign. Large sums of money are needed to win races—especially as one moves toward the highly coveted regional, state, and national seats. With large donations comes control.

Another obstacle for truly independent candidates is the power wielded by the controlled media to assist in either the promotion or demise of any candidate at any level by exploiting the amount and type of coverage provided. Once in office, there are many enticements outside of loyalty to constituents to which politicians can fall prey.

Nonprofit Organizations

Organizations are powerful sources of trust that appear as unbiased groups working on behalf of the public interest in the realms of politics, academia, law, medicine, science, business, and local communities. Their authority is related to their notoriety and length of service to society.

External funding and leadership capture are the two main avenues used to subvert original charters and position them for meaningful use in propaganda efforts. Infiltrating a Board of Directors and capturing a few key leadership positions can shift a historically strong and trustworthy organization away from its original mission.

As we have already seen, any advocacy group, even those newly created, garner trust from society because they are positioned to offer some benefit to the community at large, appear neutral and are typically thought to represent unbiased sources of information.

Justice System

The legal system can be counted on for doing its part in Operation Spider's Web by appointing corrupt or compromised judges who produce rulings that favor an agenda or support a preferred narrative. Judges are generally immune from reprisals and job termination since many are appointed for life.

They can also be used as a firewall by preventing the reversal of legal challenges that are sure to come after enacting poor legislation or by protecting the elite from criminal prosecution.

Legal training can be corrupted with "bad" money used to steer the philosophic underpinning of law schools away from a constitutional foundation and toward a progressive legal context influencing the next generation of lawyers and judges.

Science

Science is as dependent on funding as a baby is on its mother's milk. The direction of science and scientists themselves are utterly dependent on large grants and the funders of those grants. Research is expensive. Each year, billions of dollars are spent on lab equipment, materials, and man-hours. Scientists who do not get funded through grants and endowments are not likely to remain scientists. If money can't be secured for research, then good and valuable ideas get buried. He who controls the money controls the science.

Increasingly, many journals are beholden to outside funding, which influences what research projects get published. This is the exact control system that corrupted the social sciences in the 50s.

For more detailed information on the corruption of science, check out *Plague of Corruption* by Judy Mikovits and *The Real Anthony Fauci: Bill Gates, Big Pharma, and the Global War on Democracy and Public Health* by Robert F. Kennedy Jr.

Government and Regulatory Agencies

As we learned through Walter Lippmann, progressive intellectuals were advocates of having disinterested experts mold and shape society. From 1960 to 2012, the federal budget grew from 679 billion to 3.4 trillion, increased from thirteen to seventy agencies, and the pages in the Code of Federal Regulations mushroomed from 22, 877 to 174,545. Many of these agencies have powers that the founders of the constitution never intended.

A revolving door between many of the regulatory agencies with the industries under their supervision has made accountability to the people a joke. The proposed 2022 government annual budget has ballooned to 131 billion in discretionary spending and 1.5 trillion in mandatory funding, with an average of 30–50% of the proportion of each state's budget depending on federal funds returning with strings attached. That's a lot of fiscal and ultimately ideological control being mandated centrally.

For more detailed information outlining the issues of corruption and overreach in the federal government, I highly recommend Charles Murray's book *By the People: Rebuilding Liberty Without Permission.*

THE MODEL EXPLAINED

The societal institutions are depicted as light grey circles and are arranged around the media complex. Foundation money flows to those institutions with a white border while investment and corporate money control the other institutions. While I have not discussed government money specifically, it functions very much like foundation money. Federal taxes collected from individuals are returned to the states with policy strings attached which is another aspect of ideological corruption. Many of the foundation personnel shift back and forth from private work to government work, lending stability to the orthodoxy generated in the universities.

Surrounding the societal institutions are the major policy organizations of the elites described by Phillips in *Giants: The Global Power Elite*. These policy organizations are comprised of the chosen from elite universities, corporate CEOs, financial elite, politicians and agents of big tech who meet with the intention of strategizing and steering geopolitics.

Historically, meetings have been shrouded in secrecy because of the legitimate sanction against politicians engaging in secret negotiations outside the purview of the public. Somewhere along the way meetings nonchalantly emerged from behind the veil and are now routinely covered by the media, who have shifted gears seamlessly from conspiracy theory mongering to much ado about nothing.

Each small circle within a circle represents super-organizations within a given professional realm that act and speak on behalf of the entire group—even though they may or may not accurately represent them. As Wormser was able to demonstrate, Foundation personnel were able to wrest control and direction of an entire field of inquiry away from the professional themselves by means of intermediaries or clearinghouses that coordinated funding and engaged in large-scale projects that set the ideological scaffolding from which scientists and professionals are forced to navigate or languish in the system. Scaffolding is the structure surrounding the frame of the building. Once erected, it is impossible to build outside the framework. The shape and final look of the house are already determined.

The facemask icon marks those groups that use front groups extensively to affect the public opinion directly, and a spider representing the multinational PR firms sits on the web depicting the connectedness of global public relations campaigns. Please take a closer look at the model and feel free to send comments and feedback as this is a working model to pictorially represent the complex networks that undergird the creation of a false

OPERATION SPIDER'S WEB
A False Reality

reality.

THE PATH OF HISTORY

While I haven't added a ton of specific details in certain areas, I have tried to keep circling back to the singular theme of understanding propaganda from a historical timeline rather than a single point in history. In many ways, the arc of 20th-century history can be viewed as a series of monopolistic takeovers of various sectors of a once healthy society through the consolidation of wolves who realized that hunting as a pack while wearing sheepskin was much more effective and would translate them to their goals much more quickly.

In the early 20th century, the battle was on for monopolization of industry, oil, the railroads, automobiles and more. By 1913 that push gave way to the monopolization of the financial system with the passage of The Federal Reserve Act. Overlapping these battles was the fierce fight for the media; the capture of ownership, the consolidation of newspapers, magazines, television, and the invention of the Associated Press—the ultimate workaround to the serious objections an obvious media monopoly would have caused.

With the media in their pocket, the wolves could now utilize the Operation Sheepskin playbook repeatedly as they transformed society in a way that consolidated their own wealth and power.

They facilitated the rise of the propaganda machine from infancy as the exclusive domain of a few opportunistic entities wealthy enough to deploy large-scale campaigns into a powerhouse of psychic potential capable of manipulating public opinion with near scientific precision—scripting acceptable solutions to problems as cover for outright crimes.

There was no rescue on the horizon by the political class against this power as national politics degenerated into power politics; the creation of a uni-party backing big business, unions, creeping government regulations and rubber stamping the interests of the wolf cartel—selling out the people who paid the bills and cast their votes time and again. Debate was retired in preference for its malformed propaganda twins—slogan and platitude. After which true political discourse essentially ceased.

Corruption of the critical infrastructure of the United States had been completed by mid-century. This is what Mills asserted in his classic, *The Power Elite*, written in 1956. A few years later, the Kennedy assassination placed an exclamation point on the reality that mob rule had emerged, and the wolves were now in charge. The foundation of the United States was essentially rotted; it would only be a matter of time before the actual structure toppled.

The real story of the latter half of the century has been the

PROPAGANDA ERAS
Consolidation of Wealth, Resources, and Power

1900 to World War I	World War I to Kennedy Assassination	Kennedy Assassination to 9/11	9/11 to present
PIONEER ERA	WOLFPACK ERA	CONSOLIDATION ERA	GLOBALIZATION ERA
Fledgling Campaigns	Operation Sheepskin	Operation Sheepskin-Spider's Web	Operation Spider's Web
Limited Channels	Multi-Channels	Systematic Country Capture	Pseudo-Realities
Single Entity Use	Coordinated Campaigns	Media Capture Complete	24/7 Multinational Propaganda
Incomplete Media Capture	Media Capture Strong	Idea Syndicate Growing	Sclerotic Ideological Framework Established
Rise of Stagecraft	Problem | Reaction | Solution	Front Groups Explode in Number	Rise of Censorship
Marketplace of Ideas: A Battlefield	Idea Syndicate Starts		Rise of a New World Order
	US Control Established		

rise of global monopolization, global corporations, global wars, global infrastructure like the United Nations, The WHO, The World Bank, The World Economic Forum, global propaganda, and the emergence of the global citizen. Most Americans have simply been too preoccupied or lazy to notice or care.

Interestingly, this approach to expanding centralization is completely opposite to all large conquests in history, which were defined almost exclusively by military victories followed quickly by the installation of a governance structure backed by force.

So as we approach the quarter mark of a new century, where is all this headed? Is it possible to execute a global coup without violence, an iron fist concealed in a velvet glove? Is it possible to sell paradise . . . The politics of paradise? Crazy, right?

Well, if it were, I'm not sure that it could be packaged and sold any better than the campaign that is now underway.

Currently, we are witnessing a global takeover disguised as a mission of love worthy of the Queen of Charity herself— Mother Theresa. The tip of the spear in this global takeover is a massive worldwide technologically sophisticated propaganda and public relations campaign being pushed out through all the main arteries of society and carried to the smallest and most obscure capillaries.

PLANETARY PROPAGANDA

If you don't know about the 17 SDGs or sustainable development goals created and endorsed by the United Nations to supersede the Millennium Development Goals that ended in 2015—you should. The global goals are a "blueprint to achieve a better and more sustainable future for all." They are targeted to be accomplished in 2030 and were adopted by 193 countries in September 2015 in a United Nations General Assembly resolution entitled, "Transforming our world: the 2030 Agenda for Sustainable Development. You don't just wake up one day and decide to transform the world.

Eighteen months prior to the vote, devotees were working feverishly to create a monitoring framework of indicators for the SDGs—after all, what good are goals if you don't have a way to assess compliance or achievement?

Thousands of experts from UN organizations, academia, civil society, business and national statistical offices collaborated in intense global discussions on what indicators would be chosen; the seventeen goals had already been preselected somewhere deep in the bowels of the UN or some secret vault.

To accomplish such an auspicious tracking system would require a data revolution. The price tag? A mere billion a year for a robust SDG monitoring, with half to be raised through domestic resource mobilization [code word for taxes] and the rest through Official Development Assistance or ODA [code word for more taxes].

The establishment of tracking indicators for each of the goals has spawned a plethora of nonprofits devoted to delivering timely progress reports on major stakeholders tasked with carrying out the vision in every nook and cranny of the globe; corporations, universities, schools, countries, states and even a local city near you.

The main players are the Goalkeepers, SDG Alliance, The UN Sustainable Development Solutions Network (or SDSN), The World Benchmarking Alliance, The Times Higher Education Impact 2030 Rankings for all Major Universities and The SDG Index ranking the nations and individual states (see us-states.sdgindex.org).

It's important to stop now and actually look up any of the above-mentioned and observe for yourself the gigantic management tool that has already staked claim to being the arbiters of paradise defined and paradise subsequently achieved—a global report card to usher in a global paradise.

Let's see exactly what paradise looks like . . .

The 17 SDGs are: No Poverty; Zero Hunger; Good Health and Well-Being; Quality Education, Gender Equality; Clean Water and Sanitation; Affordable and Clean Energy; Decent Work and Economic Growth; Industry, Innovation and Infrastructure; Reduced Inequality; Sustainable Cities and Communities; Responsible Consumption and Production; Climate Action; Life below Water; Life on Land; Peace, Justice, and Strong Institutions; Partnerships for the Goals.

Who can argue with that? Imagine—the complete resolution of human misery accomplished by 2030.

It truly is the politics of paradise, and it is very dangerous.

Financing paradise, however, might be a bit problematic. The trillions needed hit a snag on the COVID -19 pandemic, which found governments around the world throwing money out the door into their respective economies like drunken sailors.

In light of the dilemma, a recent report by SDSN offered up a global plan to finance the development goals in six easy steps; increased domestic tax revenues, increased borrowing from multilateral development banks, sovereign borrowing on international capital markets, increased ODA [more money from your tax dollars], increased philanthropic giving and debt restructuring for heavily indebted countries.

According to this report, taxes as a percentage of GDP should be raised to 40% or higher. Currently, tax revenue in the United States is 25.5% of GDP.[82]

And if you can't raise taxes like in the developing nations, your choice is to borrow money and become a debt slave. Of course, the billionaires will throw in a few bucks, and we're all good to go.

In the midst of inflation, supply chain shortages and pressure on the world's food and energy supplies due to the conflict in Ukraine, I'm not so sure the sheep are voting for this if asked.

But it matters not. It is being rolled out behind what I

---

82. https://www.oecd.org/tax/revenue-statistics-united-states.pdf.

would call the largest, most sophisticated PR campaign in the history of the world, the hub of which appears to be an entity aptly called Project Everyone.

It would be easy to dismiss this as so much utopian nonsense—since when have UN Goals affected my life?—except that it has imperceptibly become the thematic scaffolding of the societal institutions surrounding us, shaping our environments each and every day. Exaggeration, you say?

The coordinated campaign includes a massive emphasis to indoctrinate the young worldwide through schooling and the use of sophisticated marketing materials that can be found

at globalgoals.org/resources and the World's Largest Lesson. These are slick and clever, and they are going to be effective unless we wake up. Still not convinced?

I haven't even begun to mention the wholesale adoption of SDGs by the multinational corporations. Project Everyone lists major corporate partners that have adopted one singular goal to lead by example; Unilever, for example, adopted Goal 10—Reduce Inequalities, and Google adopted Goal

5—Gender Equality.

Numerous entities like SDG Compass, UN Global Compact, Meaningful Business, the B Team, and the World Business Council on Sustainable Development have emerged as resources to hold multinational corporations accountable as they are challenged to move beyond predatory capitalism and into the role of community benefactors.

Impact 2030 exists to convince millions of corporate employees to become community SDG evangelists spreading the goodness in a new and fresh wave of local volunteerism. Should you want to learn more, the flagship education platform of the Sustainable Development Solutions Network (SDSN) is an open-source learning center called SDG Academy, offered as a resource for the public good.

And last but not least, don't forget the foundations. The 17 Rooms Initiative was first launched by the Brookings Institute and the Rockefeller Foundation in 2018 as an experiment in stimulating new forms of collective action for the SDGs. Each room or group of experts is given a focus and tasked with developing an action plan. The ubiquitous Bill and Melinda Gates Foundation sponsors the Goalkeepers site and, in cooperation with UNICEF, is funding "Project Everyone."[83]

The coordinated branding across many of these diverse platforms gives you an idea of the enormity of the public relations campaign.

As you can see, virtually everyone's been invited to the dance . . . but you and me. While the average person may have heard the term "sustainable development," few have any idea of the massive capital and man-hours already allocated to this radically transformative ideology being seeded across continents.

No one asked the sheep—they'll be sold the vision like

---

83. https://www.rockefellerfoundation.org/wp-content/uploads/2021/11/Coming-Together-Forging-New-Paths-to-Action-for-the-Sustainable-Development-Goals-17-Rooms-2021-Report.pdf.

everything else in the twenty-first century. The tribal elders have announced the problems to be solved, the measuring sticks for progress are now available, and there is very little left to do but continue to make the problems manifest (experience), trot out the talking heads leading us to predetermined solutions (authority) and castigate the deniers (social pressure). Here sheepy-sheepy.

As is always the case of things that sound too good to be true . . . the devil is in the details, as we saw looking deeper into the funding. But don't worry about all that. Don't worry about the vastly different competing interests represented across countries and cultures.

Don't ask questions; simply look at the pretty packaging, see the familiar branding all around you, hear the nice story of everybody working together to save the planet and tap into your inner hopes and dreams for a better world. What could go wrong?

Oh, and by the way—should you attempt to oppose the SDGs, you'll be giving your opponent the perfect opportunity to smear you as anti-humanity and anti-planet easily painting a target on your back.

In five to ten years, opposition to this ideological straight jacket will be suicidal.

But there is still time!

Summary

Having seized the moral high ground yet again, the wolves are salivating at the thought of world dominance. Promoting counter ideas, the very seeds of intellectual life will be nearly impossible through the rigid ideological scaffolding which is being erected around us. Counter ideas may once again need to be spread neighbor to neighbor through word of mouth and written material passed along from one to the other.

If you are new to reading the tea leaves of propaganda, this may seem far-fetched. It may seem impossible that this level of corruption exists, but you must not look away. Delve into this for yourself, and you will certainly find the truth—even though it is difficult to reconcile with your previous version of America 1.0.

The naive continue to trust leaders and institutions, blind to the vast changes that have occurred almost imperceptibly over the past one hundred years, while citizens alert to propaganda dangers and paying attention to corruption are waking up daily. They are now left with the unenviable task of trying to reverse "the spell" under which neighbors, family, and loved ones have been placed.

You now understand why facts alone don't work.

So far, we have been able to define how Operation Sheepskin and Operation Spider's Web capitalize on three of the five pillars of belief: experience, authority, and social pressure. The defining feature is some shared experience around which a story is created. Corrupted authorities then reinforce the false reality, and as the narrative is repeated and affirmed in all directions, social pressure exerts more and more force until resistance is nearly futile for the average Joe minding his own business.

The fact that these pillars are central to the execution of Operation Sheepskin and Operation Spider's Web does not diminish the power of imagination and language. In fact, language is so important that we're going to devote the entire next chapter to an in-depth analysis.

Chapter 9

WAR OF WORDS

The skilled propagandist knows the immense power of words. Those of us seeking to truly understand what we are up against and to be equipped for battle must deep dive into the action of words upon society, their correspondence with reality, the search for truth, and how they have been systematically corrupted and weaponized against Western culture and humanity in general.

In this chapter, we'll dive deeper into the amazing and vastly underappreciated importance of language as a repository of trust, as a conservator of value and a critical component of cultural cohesiveness, as first mentioned in Chapter 6. The four ways that language can be corrupted can be categorized as follows:

1. **War Over Direction:** The persuasive power of words is channeled away from an agreed-upon cultural hierarchy of values toward lesser goods or rendered dormant through neutral language.

In the beginning was the Word.
—JOHN 1:1

2. **War Over Reality:** Reality can be altered by removing words from common usage, replacing some words with others that signify different realities, or by intentionally changing the meanings of important words in common usage and thereby corrupting their original meaning.

3. **War Over Definition**: Words can be used to define a new category that competes with other generally agreed-upon categories. They can also be used to label an opponent inaccurately before he can define himself. And finally, powerful words that are vaguely defined in the public's imagination can be used falsely in order to promote opposite realities.

4. **War Over Relationships:** Corruption of the relationship that true communication requires takes place when the other person who is spoken to ceases to be a coequal partner in the quest for truth but instead is manipulated for selfish purposes.

Analyzing the thirteen-word response by Dr. Stella Immanuel to an arrogant reporter who was covering a press conference on the benefits of hydroxychloroquine in the fight against COVID-19 is a good place to start.

Hydroxychloroquine has been repeatedly maligned in the national media for being ineffective or potentially harmful to patients, despite its decades-long low-risk safety profile, and it was "on trial" in America.

As one of America's frontline doctors, Dr. Immanuel had just testified as to the beneficial effects of using HCQ with her COVID-19 patients—keeping all but a few of them out of the hospital and managing to keep all of them alive.

A reporter leaned in toward Dr. Immanuel in a mocking and intimidating manner after the conference and asked, "Aren't you afraid of losing your license to practice?" Dr. Immanuel leaned forward and asked, "How many patients should I let die, so I can keep my license?"

With one question, Dr. Immanuel had captured the moral high ground by reframing the issue with the moral seriousness that it deserved, and as a result, she sent the reporter fleeing.

A powerful thirteen words later, she had exposed and trivialized the reporter's narrow moral framework ("look after yourself"), having replaced it with her own Christian worldview of doing good to a neighbor (her patient) regardless of the cost.

She embodied the moral expectation that most of us hold, namely that doctors should not stand by and allow their patients to die while potentially life-saving drugs are left on the shelf simply because they feared retribution from bureaucrats or derision from the media.

By implication, she also condemned all the doctors who were acting in such a craven and contemptible manner.

THE WAR OVER DIRECTION

To understand the power of rhetoric, it is important to step back and examine the nature of man. In classical thought, the soul is seen as immortal and ever moving with an impulse or tendency to seek direction and orientation in a world full of meaning.

> *The education of the soul is not a process of bringing it into correspondence with the physical structure like the extended world but of **rightly affecting its motion**.*[84]

Put another way; man feels lost without a hierarchy of values and a sense of direction.

---

84. Richard Weaver, *The Ethics of Rhetoric*, (New York, 1953) 17.

*It is the nature of the conscious life of man to revolve around some concept of value. So true is this that when the concept is withdrawn, or when it is forced into competition with another concept, **the human being suffers an almost intolerable sense of being lost.** He has to know where he is in the ideological cosmos in order to coordinate his activities. Probably the greatest cruelty which can be inflicted upon the psychic man is this deprivation of a sense of tendency. Accordingly every age, including those of rudest cultivation, sets up some kind of sign post.*[85]

Thus, it is impossible to talk about rhetoric without the acceptance of a hierarchy of values and a notion of the highest good. Through her careful choice of words, Dr. Immanuel pointed to a higher order of value by contrasting love of self with love of neighbor.

True rhetoric is concerned with the potency of things, not simply with what is, but with what is possible through human imagination and effort. Therefore, rhetoric at its finest seeks to perfect men by pointing them toward something better.

At this point, let's make a distinction between true rhetoric and "base rhetoric." True rhetoric points people in the direction of the highest good—things like truth, justice, beauty, and love. Base rhetoric, on the other hand, points people in a direction that serves the purposes of others. Clearly, an open appeal to serve the interests of others will be rejected—unless it can be disguised as something noble.

It is no accident that traditional university courses in rhetoric were ruthlessly culled from academia in the mid-1900s in favor of scientific speech.

Following WWII, labeling all discourse that had emotional appeal as "propaganda" created a broad current of dislike toward

85. Ibid, 213.

all manner of rhetorical speech. The knee-jerk reaction to reject rhetoric was a classic case of throwing the baby out with the bath water. The populace would henceforth be ignorant of the revolutionary power of words and the ancient art of their use.

The critical importance of this shift away from rhetorical instruction in the academy was not lost on conservative author Richard Weaver.

> *In this loss of accreditation by rhetoric, we are witnessing one of the chief phases of modern disintegration, and those who aid and abet it are among the **leading saboteurs of our culture**. The effect of their work is to dissolve the cohesiveness that holds a culture together and to collapse the necessary hierarchy of values. **In doing this they are preparing us for a defeat by these who have not thus lost sight of the human condition.**[86]*

Cultures have a defined hierarchy of values. Using speech to point people in the direction of competing values is essentially undermining the culture, although not through weapons of war. Weaver is correct—you *can* collapse the culture by redirecting the passions of the target population.

Being able to identify and observe shifts in the hierarchy of values for a given culture is an important strategy in detecting disintegration. This is done by identifying the rhetorical absolutes—terms to which the highest respect is paid, commonly called "god terms," with the terms of reproach commonly called "devil terms."

The god terms are those expressions to which all other expressions are considered subordinate. These terms confer the greatest blessing in society and to apply a useful test—whose antonym carries the greatest rebuke. Attributes encompassed

86. Smith, 336.

in the terms attract veneration and are almost considered self-evident once embedded into the culture.

By contrast, devil terms are terms of repulsion which draw expressions of scorn, contempt, or hatred. In the public square, these labels are used to mock, ridicule, castigate, and shame.

In the mid-1900s, terms such as progress, American, modern, patriot, capitalism, science, and facts were all respected and revered in American culture. Some of the devil terms included un-American, communist, prejudice, racist, unscientific, and socialist.

Since that time, "science" and "fact" have retained their elevated status and perhaps achieved even greater veneration as the dominant source of knowledge in society by fully displacing appeals to religion and truth.

I submit the following as the current god/devil terms defining discussion in the public square and something like the present cultural hierarchy of values. These terms are grouped into three separate categories; the first is "What constitutes legitimate knowledge in society?" in other words, "Where can truth be found?" The second and third groups of terms describe the moral demands imposed on citizens who are believers in legitimate knowledge.

Highlighted terms are the ones that stand out as being the most significant in each of the categories, although in some cases, two have been selected.

God Terms

What Constitutes Legitimate Knowledge: "**Scienc**e" is the ultimate arbiter of truth in the modern world. To be **"woke"** is to be accepted among the fully enlightened ones who obey what "science" says. "Fact/Fact-checked" and "Verified" are considered synonymous with truth.

Moral Demand: Love of Planet: The following terms are used to describe people, techniques, technology and politics that are implicitly considered as desirable and life-sustaining for planet earth. **"Green,"** "Climate Change," "Sustainable," and "Smart."

Moral Demand: Love of Fellow Man: The terms **"tolerance" and "equality"** define the essence of what this modern love looks like. The terms "Global Citizen," "Fairness," "Diversity," "Social Justice," and "Black Lives Matter" are venerated sub-terms that guide modern man toward what is acceptable behavior toward others.

Devil Terms

What Does Not Constitute Legitimate Knowledge: **"Anti-Science"** is the broadest heading under which the other terms of reprobation could be included like "COVID-19 Deniers," "Anti-Vax/Vaccine Deniers," terms like "Fake News," and "Conspiracy Theorist/Conspiracy Theory" are simply creative ways of calling out what are deemed to be lies.

Moral Demands to Planet Ignored: Terms like **"Climate Change Denier,"** "Anti-Green," "Anti-Environmentalism," and "Anti-Sustainable" are, by implication, those who do not love the earth properly.

Moral Demands of Fellowmen Ignored: The terms **"Racist"** and **"Fascist"** are the broadest terms encompassing the idea of narrowmindedness, bigotry or intolerance. Other terms like "Homophobe," "White Supremacist," "Nationalist/Nationalism," "Domestic Terrorist," "Anti-immigration," "Hate Groups," or **"Nazi"** are collectively names that deride and castigate other groups or ideas for their intolerance and/or lack of inclusiveness.

When laid out in this manner, it becomes obvious that a materialist religion of sorts is being enshrined by the priests of the culture. Science and fact serve as the sacred text, revealing the truths that must be followed. Love of planet and sentimental uncritical love of others and equality are its moral demands that the woke must offer as a sacrifice to those demands, just as surely as in any religion.

Historical "facts" form the basis for the claim that American society is not just racist but filled with systemic racism since the country's founding. One certain set of facts that focus on inequality of outcomes for minorities and the oppressed is always highlighted. In this particular view of America's problems, the dominant white racist majority is always to blame. It is incumbent upon the "woke" to sacrifice for a more just society and a redistribution of the economic and political power structures. Demands must be made of the state for wholesale changes to solve the glaring inequalities.

Science is also used as the pretense for the acceptance and toleration of all claims about sexual orientation and gender fluidity. Because these are simply normal variants, toleration, fairness, and equity are demanded.

Loving the planet inevitably involves making sacrifices to save planet earth. This entails limiting consumerism, eating less or no meat, cutting one's carbon footprint, buying electric cars and so on.

As Weaver notes, "The capacity to demand sacrifice is probably the surest indicator of the god term or terms,"[87] and there is plenty of sacrifice being demanded.

Ironically, in an almost exclusively materialistic culture, the god terms have essentially come to represent a religion that has captured the moral high ground—away from Christianity, which it has soundly displaced.

87. Weaver, 214.

It is breathtaking to observe how American religious constitutional conservatives, once the bulwark of American society, have been negatively defined and represented as "the cultural enemy." Seen through devil terms, they are therefore hated and reviled—a stunning turnaround in a relatively short period of time.

Weaver notes that "there seems indeed to be some obscure psychic law which compels every nation to have in its national imagination an enemy. Perhaps the truth is that we need the enemy in order to define ourselves."[88] Since the early 1900s, America's enemies have been Germans, Nazis, USSR, communists in general, Islamic terrorists, and now domestic terrorists.

American Christians, instrumental in establishing the seminal American ethos, are now framed as narrow, selfish, greedy, racist, and anti-intellectual. Such is the power of rhetorical absolutes and the cultural hierarchy of values when they can be infused from the top down through media, Hollywood, and education.

This new cultural hierarchy has the power to direct and orient members of the community. According to your moral compass, this might be considered true rhetoric or base which orients toward things that are not truly moral goods. In the absence of true rhetoric, there is speech that fails to move the listener at all. Its goal is to stay prudent and objective, to instruct in a neutral manner, and not to excite direction. This is benign and sanitized language.

And finally, there is harmful rhetoric that attempts to motivate the listener toward the speaker's own will and to manipulate him for purposes that do not have his best interests in mind. This is the essence of propaganda and the basis for which there will be more to say later.

88. Ibid, 222.

So far, we have been considering the power of language to direct and orient. But now, let's consider two other important elements of language.

THE WAR OVER REALITY

Josef Pieper, a Thomas scholar, wrote a small book entitled *Abuse of Language, Abuse of Power* (1972) that was translated into English in 1992. Pieper plumbs the depths of classical Western thought and mines an understanding of language and power that is pure gold.

Broadly speaking, Pieper defines authentic communication as consisting of two critical elements: 1) a message about reality/truth that is 2) directed toward another human being.

> *First, words convey reality. We speak in order to name and identify something that is real, to identify it for someone, of course—and this points to the second aspect in question, the interpersonal character of human speech.*[89]

While this might seem a bit abstract, it is key to understanding and fighting back against propaganda and the tyranny that emerges with it.

To clarify what the phrase "words convey reality" means, here is an example: As a result of the growing acceptance of Darwinian theory in the late 1800s, a discipline of study emerged called the "social sciences." Darwinians believed man to be a creature of evolution, not a creation of God. They wanted to study man without reference to God. The study of man and his pursuits had previously been the exclusive domain of the humanities and religion.

This was a tectonic shift in ideology, and the lexicon of

89. Josef Pieper, *Abuse of Language, Abuse of Power*, (California, 1974, 1992), 15.

words related to man and his pursuits was soon drastically altered. "Personality" replaced "character," and the total shift toward neutrality was in full gear. Any words that still reflected "man made in the image of God" as well as words that made reference to that God were ruthlessly culled.

Character-related terms that were laden with moral connotations such as patience, temperance, malice, greed, lascivious (driven by lust), gluttony, fornication, and virtue were abandoned in favor of neutral words in order to describe man's personality without reference to God.

"Patience" was replaced by "low frustration tolerance," "virtue" changed to "pro-social" behavior, and "gluttony" gave way to the idea that obesity is genetically predetermined instead of under personal self-control. Other words like "greed," "temperance," "lasciviousness," and "malice" fell out of favor and out of common usage.

The first set of words convey a God-centered reality, and the second set of words convey a man-centered reality. Changing the lexicon of words with which to discuss man and his pursuits from God-centered to man-centered has resulted in dramatic cultural shifts. The result comes from assigning man's personal failures to cultural and environmental explanations and away from personal and eternal responsibilities.

Here we can see that the seemingly trivial displacement of one set of words for another can have a profound impact. In essence, words really do matter because both realities cannot be true at the same time.

Without words to accurately reflect an underlying aspect of reality, in many cases, an accurate understanding of that reality is in danger of being lost without a shot being fired. Words are truly revolutionary.

Orwell alludes to the powerful relationship between words and reality in the following passage from *1984,* a dystopian novel he wrote in 1948. Syme, the philologist who is a specialist in "Newspeak" is tasked with writing a new dictionary and is explaining the process to his friend Winston.

> *Do you know that Newspeak is the only language in the world whose vocabulary gets smaller every year? . . . Don't you see that the whole aim of Newspeak is to narrow the range of thought? In the end we shall make thought crime literally impossible, because there will be no words in which to express it.*[90]

In other words, an idea may exist in the mind of a man, but remain there for want of expression. Conversely, an expanded vocabulary enables sharing of highly complex ideas.

Words and language are the tools with which we convey a deep understanding of the world around us. Even the most benign conversations are a quest for truth and agreed-upon realities exert profound influence on society and goal-directed behavior.

This brings us to the second of Pieper's central ideas about human language, namely, that the words are to be spoken to someone in particular. Together, a dialogue takes place based on mutual respect and a mutual search for truth by people who are on equal footing.

But if thought corrupts language, language can also corrupt thought.
—GEORGE ORWELL, *1984*

THE WAR OVER RELATIONSHIP

When words are spoken and language used in the service of an ulterior motive without regard to truth, the person spoken to becomes an object to be manipulated, controlled, or possibly even dominated. Within this corrupt relationship, the speaker looks for weaknesses and ways to appeal so that he can further his own purposes through the communication.

90. George Orwell, *1984*, (New York, 1949), 52.

Words used in this way cease to communicate anything of value but only to manipulate. "The word is perverted and debased to become a catalyst, a drug, as it were, and is as such administered. Instrument of power may still seem a somewhat strong term for this; still, it does not seem so farfetched any longer."[91]

TYRANNICAL RELATIONSHIP

As was learned earlier from Joseph Pieper, the abuse of language or propaganda sets up a debased relationship between the propagandist and the citizen.

In the absence of truth, there is no overarching principle with which to guide the relationship—there is only the self-interest of the propagandist. It is always a one-way relationship because there is no response from the masses back to the propagandist. There are, of course, reactions and attitude changes that the propagandist is ever monitoring—like the technician hovering over the workings of a machine in order to create the perfectly crafted public opinion.

The masses are the target. The dignity of each individual man is lost within the group as a whole. Groups of people can be isolated as targets of propaganda, but the individual remains inconsequential and irrelevant. The dignity of man is always a casualty in the service of the propagandist.

Tellingly, Hitler's first premise of leadership was that the masses were utterly contemptible, incapable of abstract thinking, and ruled by feelings and unconscious drives that could be easily manipulated. He taught that,

The driving force which has brought about the most tremendous revolutions on this earth has never been a body

91. Pieper, 22–23.

of scientific teaching . . . but always a devotion which has inspired them, and often a kind of hysteria which has urged them into action. Whoever wishes to win over the masses must know the key that will open the door of their hearts.[92]

THE WAR OVER DEFINITION

The fourth and final category of corruption is definitional. There are three elements of corruption, including vague terms, the creation of new terms that indirectly compete with old ones, and the tactic of defining and labeling your opponent before he can define himself.

One of the most basic tenets in logic and debate is the need to define terms. If a term is ambiguous or unclear, nothing further can be done until the definition is refined and agreed upon by both parties. For the propagandist, vague but powerful words (democracy, American, progress, science, etc.) that embody a sentiment larger than the term are a treasure chest of gold. Used as a shield, devious plans can be recommended on the basis of terms that can hardly be criticized, similar to the god terms. These terms are trusted by the populace and refer more to a way of life than to any one particular thing. Many questionable plans can be fraudulently marketed with vague terms.

Let's look at a different example that reveals how new definitions can have profound and unsuspected culturally destructive outcomes—even when they do not appear to be in direct competition with the culture. In the character example above, god terms used to describe man's character were exchanged for materialist terms to describe man's personality in a direct challenge to define reality.

The definition attack on culture is more of a stealth attack.

---

92. Aldous Huxley, *Brave New World Revisited*, 253.

Here is an example:

The term "hate crime" came into common usage in the 1980s. Prior to this time, crimes were categorized based upon the harm inflicted on the victim: assault battery, robbery, defamation, murder, etc.

A "hate crime" was defined as a prejudice-motivated crime that occurs when a perpetrator targets a victim because of their identification with a certain social or racial demographic like Black, Hispanic, or gay.

The authors of "hate crime" legislation sought to deter bias-motivated crime by enhancing the penalties associated with conduct that was already criminal under other laws. This added a layer of protection to marginalized and discriminated groups that others lacked.

Looking out for the marginalized of society by adopting "hate crime" legislation certainly seems to fit with Judeo-Christian culture and a harmless tweak of laws already on the books. What could possibly go wrong with such a proposal?

First of all, it is redundant to label a particular crime a "hate crime" because an element of hate or callous disregard is germane to all crimes committed against other human beings.

Second, and more importantly, such legislation opens the door to group rights—something that is contrary to the Constitution and in opposition to individual rights. The rights enshrined in the Bill of Rights include freedom of action: the right to free speech, to bear arms, to assemble, and to practice religion—and these apply to all people equally. The purpose of these rights was to set clear limitations on the government's power.

"Hate crime" legislation protects "marginalized" groups by punishing offenders more severely. Once you accept that marginalized groups need special protection, they can then be enshrined with rights that infringe on the rights of other citizens.

And so we see historically that a right not to be offended by the speech of others emerges on the horizon sooner or later. And this is followed closely by proposals to criminalize unwanted speech.

This is the inescapable arc of logic that is inevitable with the adoption of group rights. We can see that the innocently labeled "hate crime" legislation has created a group category that works to alter the reality of Western culture and the legacy of individual rights that preserve our protections from tyrannical government.

Group rights enable governments to be more arbitrary and tyrannical in picking winners and losers according to the latest preferred and protected categories. Equality under the law becomes a thing of the past.

And finally, defining your opposition and labeling that opposition before he has time to label himself, is another powerful corruption of words and language. The best and most lasting example of this technique is the origination of the term conspiracy or conspiracy theory after the assassination of John F. Kennedy to quell suspicion surrounding the official narrative of the lone gunman as supported by the Warren Commission.

CIA dispatch #1035-960 was released with the aim of providing material that countered and discredited the claims of those who were suspicious of the original government narrative.

> *Although the term "conspiracy theory" lacks any fixed definition, it does serve a fixed function. Its function, like that of the word "heresy" in medieval Europe, is to stigmatize people with beliefs which conflict with officially sanctioned or orthodox beliefs of the time and place in question.*[93]

93. https://www.tandfonline.com/doi/full/10.1080/00131857.2021.1917364.

The term is always used pejoratively as part of an ad hominem attack on the opposition without having to argue the merits of the claims. It implies that there is something inherently wrong with believing in conspiracies. This is obviously untrue historically. Wanting to personally investigate the facts for oneself is a noble trait and not a liability. It ultimately herds respectable opinion away from any suspected collusion of powerful interests, making it more likely that they will get away with it. Nothing could make them happier.

ABUSE OF LANGUAGE, ABUSE OF POWER

Surprisingly, the first signs of tyranny are not readily identified by police states, armed guards throughout the country, violent repressions of the populace, suppressions of free speech, riots, show trials for enemies of the state, or the denial of rights to assemble. Rather the first signs of tyranny are when words are converted into tools of manipulation and when culture-sabotaging word substitutions are used.

Changes in patterns of communication, language usage, and word definitions often predate more overt signs of tyranny by decades. The defining characteristic of this early alarm system is the altered relationship between leaders and followers and the debasement of words from instruments in the service of truth to means of control.

Human relationships based upon power and/or manipulation signal a profound shift in respect for the dignity of people. Pieper claims that this seed, better known as propaganda, inevitably grows into the tree of tyranny.

It would not be impossible to prove with sufficient repetition and a psychological understanding of the people concerned that a square is in fact a circle. They are mere words, and words can be molded until they clothe ideas and disguise.

—JOSEPH GOEBBELS

The abuse of political power is fundamentally connected with the sophistic [propagandist] abuse of the word, indeed, finds in it the fertile soil in which to hide and grow and get ready, so much so that the latent potential of the

totalitarian poison can be ascertained, as it were, by ob-
serving the symptom of the public abuse of language.[94]

Words, when converted into tools of manipulation, signal the coming collapse of that relationship into tyranny. Disrespect between two parties is the fertile ground in which the misuse of words is nurtured. That disrespect starts verbally and can cascade incrementally into physical violence.

The degradation, too, of man through man, alarmingly
evident in the acts of physical violence committed by
all tyrannies (concentration camps, torture), has its be-
ginning, certainly much less alarmingly, at that almost
imperceptible moment when the word loses its dignity.[95]

And this brings us to the main argument of the chapter; words are revolutionary.

All speech in which the strict standard of truth or reality
has been disregarded, stands by its nature to "serve as an
instrument in the hands of any ruler to pursue all kinds
of power schemes . . . it creates an atmosphere of epidemic
proneness and vulnerability to the reign of the tyrant."[96]

In the next chapter, we will identify some vulnerabilities to propaganda so that you can buttress your own character or thinking and make yourself less susceptible to deception.

94. Pieper, 32.
95. Ibid, 33.
96. Ibid, 30–31.

Chapter 10
PLANET VULNERABLE

TYRANNY IN A DEMOCRACY

How does one convert a democracy, or rather a republic, into a tyranny? Most people would say that it can't be done. The people are supposed to rule through their elected representatives. They work for us, right? America was set up as the ultimate bulwark against tyranny.

The founders created multiple checks and balances so that no one branch of government could become too strong. They also created two chambers of the legislature to ensure that the rights of states would not be overshadowed by simple majority rule or federal overreach.

Sure, some citizens have vague feelings that the government has become less responsive or sense that there are more bad apples in government than ever before, but the alarm switch that should trigger the potent potential of a growing tyranny never gets activated.

After all, we, the people, are still in charge. We have elections, a free press, the rule of law, the Bill of Rights, and the

Constitution in place to protect us. For most people, the solid framework of freedom still stands. The answer is to get the right people into office, and then the ship will correct itself. It's nothing to worry about.

Seeing tyranny and propaganda at work in a democracy can be hard.

Plato continually concerned himself with this question over a fifty-year career when addressing the propagandists of his time.

> *The most perfect propaganda achieves just this: that the menace is not apparent, but well-concealed. Still, it must remain visible; it must remain recognizable. At the same time, those for whom the menace is intended must nevertheless be led and eased into believing (and this is the true art!) that by acquiescing to the intimidation, they really do the reasonable thing, perhaps even what they would have wanted to do anyway.*[97]

Indeed, we saw in Chapter 4 how the entire propaganda-selling task had been changed from persuasion to creating demand. Through stagecraft and Operation Sheepskin, the masses could be easily primed to demand from the propagandist the very thing he had intended to give them all along. Who needs arm-twisting and the overt tactics of tyranny? The sheep can be led to slaughter willingly. The hidden machinations behind creating the demand and the ulterior motives in compelling the predetermined solution are never revealed and never questioned—especially with a compliant media.

---

97. Pieper, 31.

Soft Tyranny

In the mid-20th century, the roadmap of two types of tyrannies was laid out in the fictional works of Aldous Huxley in *Brave New World* and George Orwell in *1984*. The critical difference between the two tyrannies was the application of force.

In *1984*, Orwell painted a picture of an aggressive overt tyranny—complete with military police, ongoing wars, interrogations, surveillance, as well as suppression of speech, ideas, and movement. The demonstration project of this type of tyranny was on full display in the lived experiments of Nazi Germany, the Soviet Union, and communist China in the 1900s.

On the other hand, in *Brave New World*, Huxley envisioned a softer, kinder, and more subtle tyranny as a bigger threat to mankind in the future. This type of tyranny would use soft techniques such as persuasion, genetic and behavioral conditioning, drugs, and a plethora of recreational activities designed to preoccupy and distract citizens, much like the Romans used "bread and circuses."

Huxley anticipated that citizens could be conditioned to "love their servitude" or at least be blissfully unaware and apathetic to it. Citizens would forget essential freedoms and lack the recognition that their lives had been usurped for the exclusive interests of a technological society that had taken control.

Writing in 1972, Pieper warned us that propagandists can even create a "fictitious reality."

A world . . .

By the skillful and sustained use of propaganda, one can make a people see even heaven as hell or an extremely wretched life as paradise.
—Adolf Hitler

*taken over by pseudo-realities whose fictitious nature threatens to become indiscernible is truly a depressing thought . . . For the general public is being reduced to a state where people not only are **unable to discern truth but also unable to even search for truth because they are satisfied with deception and trickery** that have determined their convictions, satisfied* *with a fictitious reality created by design through the abuse of language.*[98]

The ancient art of propaganda has been transformed to include tools and digital techniques that were unimaginable in Plato's time. The propagandist's reach is now global, his technological capabilities to manipulate public opinion now unthinkable.

This is, incidentally, what Huxley termed "the final revolution."

> *The older dictators fell because they could never supply their subjects with enough bread, enough circuses, enough miracles and mysteries.* ***Nor did they possess a really effective system of mind manipulation . . .***
>
> *Under a scientific dictator, education will really work—with the result that most men and women will grow up to love their servitude and will never dream of revolution. There seems to be no good reason why a thoroughly scientific dictatorship should ever be overthrown.*[99]

As noted by Neil Postman in his book, *Amusing Ourselves to Death: Public Discourse in the Age of Show Business,* he compares and contrasts the futures presented by Huxley and Orwell:

> *What Orwell feared were those who would ban books. What Huxley feared was that there would be no reason to ban a book, for there would be no one who wanted to read one. Orwell feared those who would deprive us of*

98. Pieper, 34–35.
99. Huxley, 253.

information. Huxley feared those who would give us so much that we would be reduced to passivity and egoism.

Orwell feared that the truth would be concealed from us. Huxley feared the truth would be drowned in a sea of irrelevance. Orwell feared we would become a captive culture. Huxley feared we would become a trivial culture, preoccupied with some equivalent of the feelies, the orgy porgy, and the centrifugal bumble puppy.

As Huxley remarked in Brave New World Revisited, *the civil libertarians and rationalists who are ever on the alert to oppose tyranny "failed to take into account man's almost infinite appetite for distractions."*

In 1984, Huxley added, people are controlled by inflicting pain. In Brave New World, *they are controlled by inflicting pleasure. In short, Orwell feared that what we hate will ruin us. Huxley feared that what we love will ruin us.*[100]

THREAT AWARENESS

One of the main vulnerabilities to propaganda is the failure to acknowledge its actual far-reaching structure, its long history in America, and its continued presence in democracies.

As we learned earlier, after the war years, the word "propaganda" never recovered suitably from its exclusive association with communist and fascist societies, and so it gradually faded from use. Citizens, blind to a stealthy predator with powerful underground weaponry, go on blissfully.

---

100. Neil Postman, *Amusing Ourselves to Death: Public Discourse in the Age of Show Business*, 5.

You cannot defeat a threat you choose not to define.[101]

Another major vulnerability caused by the wholesale embrace of a materialistic world is the disappearance of the idea of evil that is always disguised as an angel of light. Deception has been mentioned over and over.

The con is to gain trust, to hide behind venerated institutions, organizations, and powerful words so that evil can be insidiously planted in the midst of what is conceived as good. This is an ancient concept that is truly lost even among Christians who cannot comprehend what has been done to their country.

You cannot defeat a threat you choose not to believe exists.

—MICHELLE STILES

KNOWLEDGE BIAS

The world as we know it is a world of things, a place of stuff to be examined under the cold glare of laboratory lights. Scientific facts are crowned as the pinnacle of knowledge. Facts dictate decisions. Trust science.

It was not always this way. In fact, our ancestors saw the world as a place of meaning and a forum for action. How one acted and who one became were more important than the simple realities of time and space. The question of whether we ought to go on living as we do was not thought of as a scientific question. Answers were to be sought in the study of the humanities, mythology, religion, the arts, history, and philosophy.

So who is right? Do we live in a world of stuff or in a world of meaning?

The answer is that both realms are vital to man's existence. In fact, there are two distinct orders of knowledge, separate but coequal. Neither should stand alone.

101. Stephen Coughlin, *Re-Remembering the Mis-Remembered Left: The Left's Strategy and Tactics to Transform America*, (Washington, DC, 2019), 150.

Examination of the material world is the domain of science and the first order of knowledge, the study of "what is."

The second order of knowledge seeks to determine proper orientation in the world or "what ought to be." What is man's highest good? How should man conduct himself? What is the meaning of life? These questions relate to orientation and values—the "shoulds" and "oughts."

One can never infer how man should act or what he should value from a detailed examination of the material world through facts, data, and science.

As Richard Weaver correctly pointed out in *The Cultural Role of Rhetoric*, "Any assumption that such questions can be answered scientifically, or even that answers can be put in purely scientific language, is subversive of social ordering, which has to have its sanction from elsewhere."[102]

Sadly, this is what has happened. Overreliance on a hyper-materialist orientation and failure to acknowledge the world of meaning and value has given rise to a culture woefully ignorant of an entire realm of knowledge that is critical for setting the overall direction of society.

We are deluded into believing that we can derive an "ought" from an "is."

Alarm bells should go off when courses of action are presented as solely derived from "facts" or "science."

102. Smith, 337.

DOMAINS OF KNOWLEDGE

MATERIAL WORLD Facts | Data | Science	SPIRITUAL WORLD Ultimate Value and Goals
What Is	What Ought to Be
Mastery	Orientation
Real	Relevant
Science	Stories of Meaning
	Myths Religion
	History Arts
	Drama Poetry

VS

The domains are separate but equally important. Facts by themselves are not enough to determine direction without a value structure.

A DESIRE FOR COMFORT AND SECURITY OVER CONFRONTATION AND RISK

Facts don't motivate people sufficiently—stories do. Stories provide meaning and orient you toward an ideal—that "this place" is better than "that place." It makes perfect sense that a culture that has lost touch with meaning, as we saw in the last section, would gravitate toward safety and security over any risk—after all, why should I risk my neck? What good reasons exist for me to wander out into the unknown without backup?

Unbearable Present ⟶ Desirable Future

All stories have the following elements:

A Knower: the main protagonist in the story.

The Known: the protagonist's current situation.

The Unknown: that which the protagonist must encounter and surmount to obtain a better life or a higher state of existence.

The basic elements of a story mirror the elements found in all great myths.

Each of the basic elements has positive and negative aspects. Despite the current low view of myths being something primitive or ignorant, in reality, archetypes represent a sophisticated and insightful rendering of the complexity of our lives in the habitable world. We touched on this briefly in Chapter 7, and now we're going to delve a bit deeper.

The Great Father (Order and Tyranny) is a symbol sometimes used in mythology to represent explored or known territory. This is the place where we are secure in familiar surroundings, where human behavior has been rendered predictable, and where the course of "natural" events can be accurately determined. It represents home ground, culture or society.

The positive aspect of the known is that it provides structure, order, and security, without which culture and cooperation in society could not exist. The negative aspect of the known is that it can be corrupted into tyranny. A paradox exists between order and tyranny because security of person and property is always obtained at the cost of freedom. This creates a constant tension between the two poles of *Known Territory*.

The Great Mother (Creation and Destruction) is a symbol sometimes used in mythology to represent unexplored or unknown territory. This territory is the source of all new knowledge but can be dangerous and destructive. This, too, is paradoxical because creation and destruction are integrally linked—the old must be destroyed to give way to the new. Cycles of life emerge from death and rebirth. The unknown compels curiosity but also terror because death and destruction are real possibilities when venturing forth.

The Hostile Brothers (The Hero and the Adversary) are examples of the archetypical response to the unknown. The hero confronts change. He ventures into the unknown with courage and faith that it will bring renewal and redemption. Every success brings knowledge. This strengthens his character as success imbues confidence. This results in being constantly refreshed by living water and an updated view of the world.

The adversary resists and shrinks from everything he does not understand. This weakens his character. He is no longer nourished by renewal and regeneration, which leads him to become more and more rigid and authoritarian. Each retreat from living water increases his fear. He seeks protection but with successful protection comes frustration, boredom, and a contempt for life. There is no growth without risk, no rebirth without death.

A culture that has elevated safety and security above all else will ultimately succumb to tyranny. Orthodoxy will be elevated over variability and the free exchange of ideas. The culture becomes static, paralyzed, and hardened.

Comfort and security are preferred to venturing out into the unknown to bring new meaning, life, and challenge to society. Lacking heroes, society loses the ability to navigate incremental change and to update outdated systems and concepts that have ceased working.

This phenomenon occurs organically at first. Eventually, however, truly tyrannical states seek to censor, outlaw, demonize, and persecute the true heroes who attempt to bring living water back to the culture.

Two Sides to Every Story

Understanding the schema of mythology helps you to remember that "there are two sides to every story." The culture or governance from which you derive your stability is a wonderful thing. Imagine getting up every morning and needing to determine if the roads are clear so you can get milk or worrying whether you'll have power at home or might be attacked while traveling to work?

That same culture can allow order to be taken too far. The demand for uniformity can crush and suffocate the human spirit, making the society that refuses micro changes much more vulnerable to violent upheaval and precipitous decline.

Alternately, humans can't live forever in chaotic environments. Therefore, it is vital to value the exploration of the unknown and cherish the hero in order to sustain a life-giving culture.

It is also important to remember that the potential for hero and devil resides in each person. As Solzhenitsyn remarked about the problem of soviet tyranny:

> *If only there were evil people somewhere insidiously committing evil deeds, and it were necessary only to separate them from the rest of us and destroy them. But the line dividing good and evil cuts through the heart of every human being. And who is willing to destroy a piece of his own heart?*[103]

---

103. Aleksandr Solzhenitsyn, *The Gulag Archipelago*, (New York, 1973), 168.

Unfortunately, we no longer think in mature terms by seeking out the "other side of the story"—the balanced wisdom gleaned from understanding centuries-old mythological concepts.

Simplistic immature thinking exists on both ends of the left/right spectrum.

Right-wingers typically embrace conservatism, "The Great Father" who provides stability. Left-leaning liberals typically embrace change, "The Great Mother" who stimulates birth and creative renewal—yet both sides are needed.

Some liberals foolishly attack the foundation of the United States because they wrongly conclude that the whole society is corrupt because some of the founders owned slaves or were racist. But in fact, a sign of a healthy society is one that can change directions and make modifications like those seen during the Civil Rights era. Heroes like Martin Luther King helped make this change of direction a reality.

Conversely, some conservatives, while worshiping the foundational principles of the United States, fail to see the corruption in the current system and the parts of society that are genuinely suffering. Clearly, there has been a static hardening of corruption and a subversion of those original principles that they simply cannot see.

Both sides need to see that the corruption is deeper and more systemic and the answers far more involved than simply electing a different president.

New heroes must arise to meet the unique challenges of the present generation to confront and condemn corruption.

WRONG AIM IN LIFE

Dr. Daniel Simons, a cognitive psychologist, created a brilliant experiment demonstrating the limitations of a concentrated focus. In his gorilla experiment, Dr. Simons had participants watch a video of two teams of three people passing a ball among other team members milling about in a small area. The participants were asked to count the number of times the ball passed between members of one team.

At the end of the video, they were asked for their responses. Getting the number of passes correct was immaterial to the study. What was important was determining if the participants, while focused on the movement of the ball, had seen the person in a gorilla suit walk into the middle of the screen, beat his chest and exit. Fifty percent of the participants failed to see the gorilla.

This led to other studies that proved a similar point. Focused intent causes the eyes to dim everything else down to low resolution so that our fovea (a part of the eye) can maximize its high-resolution capabilities. In a very real sense, what you focus on determines what you see. Our minds are trained to see things that facilitate our desired goals. If our goals are faulty, we will literally be missing things of importance that could be right in front of our eyes. The bottom line is this: Choose your aim wisely because most everything else gets conceptually zeroed out.

So what on earth does this have to do with propaganda vulnerability? As we have seen, the propagandist is no dummy. His goal is to offer you a cheap imitation of something desirable and make it look like the real thing. The politicians and corporations want you to believe that they have your best interests at heart (trust) instead of consolidating their own money and power—the real objects of their desire.

Citizens whose hearts and minds are focused on comfort, safety, security, and easy living are prime targets for propaganda. Indeed, this would mean all those who have turned away from objective truth and a hierarchy of value and who have put their trust in the material world.

After the Enlightenment, the idea of a universe governed by divine providence and full of meaning was overthrown in exchange for a universe of physical laws—or was it?

Nietzsche declared that not only was God dead but that human beings had killed him with their scientific revolution. Far from declaring a victory, Nietzsche warned the world in *Twilight of the Idols:*

> *When one gives up the Christian faith, one pulls the right to Christian morality out from under one's feet. This morality is by no means self-evident . . . Christianity is a system, a whole view of things thought out together. By breaking one main concept out of it, the faith in God, one breaks the whole.*[104]

In the absence of this moral framework, Nietzsche believed that most people would be at the mercy of despair or meaninglessness. He feared this would lead to widespread pessimism or the advent of nihilism, which he correctly predicted would sweep over Europe toward a catastrophe.

Into the void of meaning, massive propaganda overtook Europe and the destructive ideologies of communism and Nazism raged in the 20th century. Pathetic attempts to restrict the meaning of life to that of a "worker" or that of a participant of a special group (a master race) had failed miserably, but not without profound consequences and the death of millions.

Nietzsche had hoped that an individual who created his own meaning by will alone, what he called the "Ubermensch" or "Superman," could arise and take the place of the Christian man and become the new moral ideal in the brave new scientific world.

In reality, Nietzsche recognized that the contemptible "Last Man" (a term he coined to describe those who live a

---

104. Friedrich Nietzsche, *Twilight of the Idols*, part 5, https://www.praxeology.net/twilight3.htm#:~:text=When%20one%20gives%20up%20the,of%20things%20thought%20out%20together.

quiet life of comfort, without thought for individuality or personal growth) was more likely to succeed in replacing the Christian man.

"We have invented happiness,"—say the last men, and they blink.[105]

TRIUMPH OF IMAGES OVER LANGUAGE

Since the advent of television, access to images has exploded, shifting man's previous reliance on language and discussion toward images for gaining knowledge and information. Because all of us have been situated in this environment since birth, it is difficult to quantify the changes that have come over us as a result.

In *The Humiliation of the Word*, Jacques Ellul calls it the greatest mutation known to humankind since the Stone Age. Ellul explains that sight orients us to the material world, the reality in which we are situated that allows us to move and act upon that world.

Spoken language, on the other hand, goes beyond the material world to enter another universe—the domain of truth that can only be expressed in language. It is the second order of knowledge that we discussed earlier in the chapter.

As a reminder, the domain of truth is anything concerned with the ultimate destination of a human being. Destination is the same as "meaning and direction in life." We can add to this everything that refers to the establishment of a hierarchy of value, allowing a person to make significant personal decisions, and everything related to the debate over justice and love and their definitions.

105. Friedrich Nietzsche, *Thus Spake Zarathustra*, 6, http://www2.hawaii.edu/~-freeman/courses/phil394/Thus%20Spoke%20Zarathustra.pdf.

Today we are witnessing the fulfillment of Edgar Allen Poe's prophecy in *The Oval Portrait,* in which the painter, awed by the image, is entirely unaware and disconnected from the actual loss of that reality.

The painter . . .

did not want to see that the colors he spread on his canvas were taken from the cheeks of the woman seated beside him. And when several weeks had passed, and very little remained to be done, nothing but a stroke on the mouth and a glaze over the eye, the mistress's spirit still flickered like a flame at the base of a lamp. Then he put on the final touch, put the glaze in place, and for a moment the painter stood in ecstasy before the work he had finished. But a moment later, he was struck with panic, and shouting with a piercing voice: "It is truly Life itself," he suddenly turned around to look at his mistress. She was dead.[106]

Nothing ever constrains us from facing what is dying when we see it as being so alive in our images.

We have come to the place where it is actually possible to keep the image alive and the idea of America via on-screen images, when in fact, the embodiment of those ideas has long since vanished.

Our civilization's major temptation is to confuse sight and images with truth. We are made to believe that sight and images are truth. Debate, reasoning, language, rhetoric, reading, discussions, and critical thinking have all been devalued by an overemphasis on images.

The image-oriented person, now an increasing majority in society, follows a different intellectual process than the one

106. Edgar Allen Poe, *The Oval Portrait* https://www.gutenberg.org/files/2147/2147-h/2147-h.htm#chap11.

developed by classical education. Images cause us to grasp facts in a comprehensive manner more akin to intuition, suggestion, and association than the critical faculties of intelligence and reason.

As we move from image to image, various emotions are stimulated—from anger to resentment, from passion to curiosity—even fear or indignation. A person raised entirely on images and barred from training in classical thinking produces a human being with a tendency toward extreme violence of conviction but who lacks supportive coherent arguments.

W. B. Yeats, in *The Second Coming*, seemed to understand exactly this danger when he penned, "The best lack all conviction, while the worst are full of passionate intensity."[107]

It can be seen all around us today in the over-the-top juvenile displays of emotion expressed by social justice warriors on behalf of their passionate convictions that they are unable to articulate. Screaming on the steps of the supreme court to express disapproval of political outcomes is the sad outworking of this mutation of intelligence.

Analogous to this are the emotionally distraught childlike reactions to "triggers"—ideas or concepts that are supposedly "offensive." Rather than embracing free speech and using one's powers of expression to refute the offensive idea, "the offense" is instead used as an emotional stimulant that is beyond refutation by childlike minds.

All this proceeds from debasement of the word and the elevation of images and emotional states above critical thinking and love of the truth.

107. W.B. Yeats, *The Second Coming*, https://www.poetryfoundation.org/poems/43290/the-second-coming

BETRAYAL BLINDNESS

No one likes to admit there are traitors in our midst nor that there have been traitors at the highest levels of our government for a long time. As a bracing shot of cold water to the face, I'm going to reach back in time to a quote from good old George Creel, who bragged . . .

> *Many a good and misinformed citizen, who had an unformed but vivid impression that the "Creel Committee" was some iniquity of the devil, took with his breakfast a daily diet of our material from the same journal that had given him this impression.*[108]

How is it possible that Creel and his committee could get material published in a journal that held the impression that the Creel committee was a tool of the devil? If they really hated the Creel committee and what it stood for, Creel's materials would be dead on arrival. What's going on?

What if the editors weren't really on the side of those who hate the Creel committee? What if they were, instead, "controlled opposition?" Can you see how powerful that would be if certain wolves had media stakes on both the right and left sides of the political aisle? They could feed politically useful information down both sides of a greased shoot while maintaining the illusion of free speech in a free society. Brilliant!

All it takes is a few good men. Men that will infiltrate both sides at the highest levels but who maintain allegiance to the wolves. Once in the circle of trusted allies, the movement is loath to believe there are traitors in its midst. It's an act of betrayal or treachery to make common cause with a movement and sell them out behind the scenes in exchange for your own power and prestige, but it sure is politically useful!

108. Creel, 109.

The same thing can be done with political candidates—groom the traitor that can be financially controlled; manipulate the primary process through campaign contributions and the media, and repeat this on both sides of the political aisle so that no matter who wins, the wolves can consolidate their capital and power.

And finally, let's say the rank and file start to get angry with the phony treacherous politicians being elected year after year and their repeated failures to follow through with campaign promises. Angst starts to build, and a genuine intra-party opposition movement starts to develop; the people's candidate emerges who is a leader for the disaffected and disenfranchised. Well, that can't happen.

The powers that be aren't dumb—let's find a treasonous "people's" candidate—one who can talk the language of true liberalism or true conservatism but who ultimately does the wolves bidding. All it takes is money and a few boot-licking men or women.

If this sounds diabolical and wicked, you are right. If you think that it could not possibly happen, you have "betrayal blindness." Creel let us in on a secret over one hundred years ago. It's the perfect plan of control to maintain the illusion of democracy.

HISTORICAL CONTEXT

Throughout this book, I have referred to "stagecraft" as planned events made to look like organic experiences designed to alter public opinion, sell merchandise, or alter public policy. I would be remiss if I did not discuss the term "false flag" as a specific type of the stagecraft phenomenon.

A false flag is a violent act committed with the intention of framing another person with responsibility (typically called a "patsy") or group (like a political party, religious organization, or terrorist group). This is done in order to smear the reputation of that group and/or to use the violence for political ends. Many times, there are government officials called "moles" whose task is to ensure that only the patsy is investigated and prosecuted or that the crime gets pinned on the intended group such that the real perpetrators get away with it. In addition, there may be what are called "agent provocateurs" who are on the side of the perpetrators in order to maneuver the patsy or group into position so that the violence can be blamed on them.

"False flag" was coined in the 16th century to describe a naval maneuver whereby a vessel would deceptively fly the flag of a neutral or non-hostile country in order to move into proximity to launch an attack on an unsuspecting ship.

Intrigue in politics is nothing new, and there have been volumes written on false flag terrorism in the service of political ends. For the purposes of this book, it is enough to recognize the term or terms associated with the typical false flag operation and to be able to identify it as a staged experience that is used to manipulate and shift public opinion in a way that benefits the perpetrators.

I have chosen not to use the term "false flag" until late in this book so as not to contaminate the broader phenomenon of using manufactured experiences to impact beliefs and behavior in multiple ways. After the war, Bernays used it successfully in sales and marketing in the service of profits for large corporations. It was and is used successfully by politicians and PR firms to stage events of significance that are nonviolent and that have the potential to draw attention and command interest.

I would argue that a manufactured event could even be extended to the phenomenon we observe in science whereby a fraudulently conducted experiment is needed and desired to create a major shift in consensus opinion or research interest.

Such a maneuver was accomplished by CDC research on early administration of the MMR vaccine to a population of mostly African-American school children in Atlanta, GA, to determine if it posed a higher risk of autism.

This was exposed in 2014 by Dr. William Thompson, a whistleblower who was part of the original study. Dr. Thompson testified that the team of researchers agreed to falsify the results to conclude that the MMR vaccine was safe when given in the timetable suggested in federal guidelines. In fact, the study showed the exact opposite—that early administration of the MMR vaccine *did* result in a significantly higher incidence of autism, but the sham conclusion was widely touted and used to funnel millions of research dollars away from further inquiry into the issue.

Ultimately, an acclaimed research paper or study can function as a manufactured event within the scientific community and among the general population with widespread circulation and promotion through the media. Instead of being seen as part of the growing body of work from which scientists draw conclusions, it is hailed as "breakthrough research" or a "definitive study." Positioning the work in this way allows for maximal impact.

The reader should learn as much history as possible and evaluate the rich literature on false flags. Learning history is like ripping the naïve label off our head and donning a bulletproof vest. If you have to remain in a herd of sheep, be in a smart herd.

Chapter 11
PROPAGANDA DETECTIVE

The truth will come out in the end. Howard E. Hunt got a bit greedy when he went after Liberty Lobby, a magazine publisher that had printed a damning article about his alleged involvement with the Kennedy assassination on November 22, 1963, as part of the CIA.

Liberty Lobby lost the first case, and Hunt was awarded a significant settlement that had the potential to put Liberty Lobby out of business. The owners hired Mark Lane, a man renowned for his detailed knowledge of the Kennedy assassination, to defend them in the appeal. The new judge, at Lane's request, tossed out an unwise pre-trial stipulation from the first trial that conceded that Hunt was not in Dallas on the fateful day of the assassination, and it was game on in the re-trial to prove that Hunt was in fact in Dallas, and was party to the CIA's actions to murder President Kennedy.

In a Florida courtroom in January 1985, Mark Lane put Hunt on the witness stand and cornered him in a lie. Hunt's alibi at the previous trial was that he was with his family in

Washington, D.C. on the day of the Kennedy assassination. Hunt admitted that he had previously alleged that his family relationships had suffered as a result of the accusations linking him with the Kennedy murder, reasoning the jury used to award him substantial damages in the first case.

Oblivious to Lane's line of questioning, Hunt was forced into an embarrassing admission. If Hunt's family had been with him in D.C., as he alleges, they would know without a shadow of a doubt that he could not have been in Dallas acting as the bag man for the murderers.

Hunt's credibility took several more broadsides before he weakly left the witness stand, but the damage was done.

After the trial, the jury concluded that the CIA had taken part in the Kennedy assassination and acquitted Liberty Lobby of libel.

This was the same Howard E. Hunt who was placed in charge of CIA forces assisting in the overthrow of Arbenz in Guatemala, the same Howard E. Hunt involved at the fringes of the Bay of Pigs and the same Howard E. Hunt convicted as a bugler during the Watergate scandal in the 70s.

It took over twenty years for this and other damning pieces of evidence to come to light. Many of the criminals at the center of this dark chapter in America's history were already dead and buried, all were now out of office, elderly and frail, hoping no one was paying attention—most of us were not.

Learn from History

For this reason, to the dustbins of history you must go to start your search for truth and the understanding of what propaganda is and how it works. The crimes of the present appear absurd and fantastical, a mere fiction without historical context.

You must go to the losers in time, the men whose stories pull back the curtain on the orthodoxy that "won" the public relations battle but killed truth in the process. These are the whistleblowers who lost lives and fortunes to stand against the tide of the great consolidation of industry and power, who stopped at nothing to achieve dominance.

It's likely that few people have heard of or remember George Eggleston despite the considerable sacrifice he made laboring in golden years to record the action of corrupt leaders who tried to silence dissent and punish him—an American, for having the nerve to stand up to power. He, as well as other good men were castigated and harassed for sharing opinions antithetical to powerful hidden forces.

Weaver wisely counseled to ally oneself with the defeated and to look "at the 'progress' of history through the eyes of those who were left behind" and that "the study and appreciation of a lost cause have some effect of turning history into philosophy."[109]

I would highly recommend starting with the three controversial but seminal events of the 20th and 21st centuries, the assassination of JFK, 9/11 and COVID-19. Each event serves as a pivot point in history and, hopefully, having read most of the way through this book, you now have a vivid understanding of the array of forces consolidating power in the marketplace of ideas since the early nineteen hundreds. Without historical context, you'll have little success plunging into current world events and "figuring things out."

Becoming your own successful propaganda detective will require practice but becomes easier and almost second nature within a short time. Additionally, I hope that this new understanding of how the marketplace of ideas has been contaminated will spur a critical inquiry into the perversion of authentic communication, leadership, and self-governance and foster open discussions of ways to combat what has morphed

109. Ted Smith, ed., *In Defense of Tradition: Collected Shorter Writings of Richard Weaver*, 1929–1963, (Indiana, 2000), 39.

into a leviathan. It's going to take more than individuals alone seeing the light to stem the tide and way more than a new election cycle to clean up the mess.

For example, how is it possible, given our reliance on the Infrastructure of Belief, to defend against its manipulation? How is it possible to safeguard ourselves against selective editing and the perversion of the truth by the news media? How can we trust authorities that are distant and whose true character is hidden?

These are difficult but important questions that need to be answered if a workable self-governing culture is going to exist. Obviously, much of this would have to start with breaking up the media monopoly as it exists today.

Mapping out the propaganda threat is the first step which is what this book is about. Secondly, become a propaganda detection wizard so that you can decode and neutralize the con game being played against you. Thirdly, spread the word and educate others. Once the spell is broken—there is no putting the con back in the box.

Let's summarize what you should be able to do with the knowledge you have gained so far.

1. Define the threat—both the system and the true menace behind it.

2. Recognize that the Infrastructure of Belief is a shortcut to knowledge in communities and the essential reason why facts and logic are not sufficient to change people's minds.

3. Recognize how each of the five pillars can be captured and utilized to shape public opinion.

4. Recognize how the Primal Architecture of the Brain makes humans susceptible to novel, disconcerting, threatening, and chaotic events or experiences.

5. Be able to identify the Operation Sheepskin pattern in society and then discern the probable goals of the "marketing campaign."

6. Be able to identify the morphing of an Operation Sheepskin event into Operation Spider's Web.

7. Become skilled at researching the personalities, superorganizations, and the money flow supporting Operation Spider's Web in order to reveal the corruption.

Behold the Jury Trial

There is one special place where determining the truth matters supremely—the courtroom. Lives hang in the balance; justice is waiting at bay, and victims crave restitution. The stakes are high-reluctant witnesses subpoenaed to ensure their appearance in court; swearing under oath to tell the truth, and threatened with jail if found lying. The jury hears both sides of the story, each of which sounds compelling.

Lawyers for each side cross-examine the witness bringing out facts and statements that the first testimony left uncovered. More witnesses are called to confirm or refute original stories or to add new details. Experts are called to testify to the veracity of the facts. Motives are examined, and a money trail is explored—who benefits from the events that took place? Thousands of dollars and months later, the decision is put in the juries' hands—more days go by. At last, a verdict—is it the truth?

While not perfect, the judicial system is a well-crafted way of getting at the truth. Does it work in all cases? Unfortunately, no, but it sure beats going before the Spanish inquisition.

Let's use this framework to our advantage by allowing it to inform our search for truth in everyday life.

The best protection against propaganda of any sort is the recognition of it for what it is. Only hidden and undetected oratory is really insidious. What reaches the heart without going through the mind is likely to bounce back and put the mind out of business. Propaganda taken in that way is like a drug you do not know you are swallowing. The effect is mysterious; you do not know afterwards why you feel or think the way you do.

—Mortimer J. Adler, *How to Read a Book: The Classic Guide to Intelligent Reading*

HEAR BOTH SIDES OF THE STORY

Beware the One-Sided Story

The world is a complex place. Just like in a good detective whodunit story, it takes time to discover the truth surrounding an event, and even then, things can remain hidden for years. Trickery and deception are ever-present, and nothing is ever as straightforward as it seems. Competing interests abound.

RED FLAG: Suspicions should be immediately aroused when the media locks onto one narrative over others.

Bad Guys Identified with Ease

Similarly, investigating the causes of something and identifying the perpetrators—separating the good guys from the bad guys takes time. [Think about how much effort it takes to referee an altercation between siblings in an argument.] It isn't easy or simple. Imagine the increased complexity of geo-political stories and the substantial number of competing interests at stake. And yet, time after time, the media is able to announce almost overnight the perpetrators to major events and have stories about them at the ready. Real investigations are never solved so quickly and cleanly. When the media presents its case, ask how likely it is that data on a person/or country suspected of wrongdoing could have been gathered so quickly. In many cases, simply using your brain in this way alerts you to deception. The goal for the media is to establish the dominant storyline before any competing storylines can take root.

RED FLAG: Perpetrators named ridiculously early in the process.

The Assumption of Truth without Debate

Affirmation is the treatment of some doctrine or opinion as if it were universally accepted dogma. Once the media narrative has been set, it is often treated as unassailable; questions or criticisms are assigned to the lore of conspiracy theory. Remember Weaver's words:

> *By this means of misrepresentation, the propagandist assumes either boldly or blandly that everyone in his right mind accepts the opinion as a necessary presupposition, and then he proceeds to build his case upon it. The effect of this maneuver is to keep the proposition, which is essential to the argument away from public criticism.*[110]

RED FLAG: *When the media affirms the narrative and then repeats it over and over without providing relevant evidence or allowing debate, there is likely deception.*

Dig deeper: Question the original narrative, examining the possible financial flows of money by seeking alternative explanations and motives.

Examine Raw Data

Early witnesses whose testimony is nonconforming to the budding narrative will be swept away and disregarded after being checked out by the FBI or some other agency. This is why it is very important to check social media for eyewitnesses' accounts of actual events early because access to those videos or testimonials may not be available later. Many citizen journalists have combed through hours of raw video data and confirmed elements of a story, which are later denied by the press. Suppression of nonconforming data is becoming routine by big tech, so early access to key elements of the story should be archived and shared.

RED FLAG: *Censorship or suppression of raw date like security camera videos, witness videos, audio recordings or even government documents, etc.*

110. Smith, 307.

Settled Science

Science is always in a state of flux and never fully settled. Anyone who tells you differently is flat-out lying. If the evidence is abundant, why censor the debate? If the case is as airtight as it is deemed to be, then provide a platform and demonstrate the error of the opposing viewpoint. Without this kind of transparency, quick-thinking people are correct to question "settled science."

Remember, science can be easily corrupted by tweaking the methodology and the statistics of any research project in order to "prove" a false concept or attempt to disprove a compelling one. It is vitally important to provide forums for any scientist or researcher to criticize the data being used to promote a narrative.

RED FLAG: *Considering science "settled" and stifling healthy debate.*

Event Sponsors

Most events are sponsored by some group or organization. Track that organization and the people working on its behalf. Who is on their board of directors? With what other organizations are they associated? Can you see a larger pattern or constellation of groups working together for one specific aim?

Protests and civil unrest by any group or organization should be evaluated in terms of the financial backers of the event. The timing of any event immediately on the heels of a crisis should raise suspicions related to the speed with which it is organized. The same is true of the strategic timing of events just prior to a crisis.

Organic grassroots organization takes time, especially when staffed by volunteers. The presence of paid protesters should immediately establish that the entire event is fraudulent. Frequently, advertisements for paid protestors can be found on Craigslist prior to an event. If arrests are made following the event, the presence of large numbers of people from out of state should also bring suspicion.

RED FLAG: Simultaneous events launched across the country take massive coordination and money. Who wants this to happen?

The Committee Subterfuge

When significant questions are raised over a given narrative, or authentic grassroots pushback emerges from within the culture, beware the formation of The Committee. The committee is a great way to assure the population that the governing powers are looking into the problem, and all is well. Meanwhile, the topic is buried in the mind of the public, and the outrage quelled. The object of the committee is either to whitewash the issue as far as is possible or offer a limited hangout of some trivial matter and bury a much more serious issue that could expose the entire charade of democracy. The Warren Commission was a perfect example of this type of bureaucratic jujitsu.

WITNESS CREDIBILITY – PERSONNEL

Just like in a courtroom, establishing witness credibility is essential in parsing out truth from lies.

If you can remember Chapter 6, when I started my journey as a propaganda detective, I was struck by an anomaly; an attractive young woman was being passed off as an expert on Syrian political issues—an unlikely scenario given what I knew about Middle Eastern male attitudes toward women.

I questioned her credibility immediately, just through common sense. I used the Internet for research and came to my own conclusions. Later, her degree status at Georgetown was investigated by another inquiring mind and found to be fraudulent, trashing her credibility and authority.

Determining the history of the main players in any historical event is critical. Corrupt players resurface again and again in different roles as trusted establishment hacks. The powers that be expect you to have a short memory and that you will forget their previous roles.

A quick look in Wikipedia (although a potential source of disinformation itself) will usually at least provide the main biographical details of a person's life. Another place to search is WikiSpooks, a site that attempts to compile data on known Deep State players.

Have these players been involved in previous cover-ups? Were they rewarded for those crimes? A prime example is Rudy Giuliani, the mayor of New York City, who presided over the rescue and recovery efforts of the twin towers after 9/11. One of the more questionable things that was done during that time was the immediate collection and transport of the scrap metal from the collapsed buildings to barges bound for China—in the absence of any investigation by fire safety inspectors—as required by law.

It is hard to imagine any honorable scenario in which such contamination of a crime scene would be allowed to take place—especially one of the magnitude of 9/11.

In addition, World Trade Center 7 was remarkably the only steel structure in modern history to collapse by fire alone. Surely that fact by itself should have required significant investigation in order to satisfy questions about the safety of all future high-rise buildings. Furthermore, the twin tower debris fields should have been rigorously evaluated by the FBI and fire safety inspectors as well in order to determine the nature of their collapse. This examination would have included the search for any potential signs of criminal activity that may have weakened the building prior to collapse.

Once you know this fact about Mayor Giuliani, it is prudent to question his true allegiance to the country and to be suspicious about his involvement in other political events.

Witness Credibility – Organization

As we have seen with Operation Spider's Web, there is a multitude of organizations spreading influence. If we are to evaluate truth, we must be able to establish an organization's credibility as well as individual credibility. Organizations aren't neutral; they cost money and effort to bring into existence and more money and effort to maintain.

Here is an example of how I dug up information on Bone Smart, a nonprofit outfit positioned as a community service organization but which was, in fact, something much different.

As a physical therapist, I was familiar with an organization called "Bone Smart." I had explored the Bone Smart website, a forum on recovery from knee replacement surgery several times previously and was uncomfortable with the advice being given. Seemingly it is run by those who had fully recovered from knee replacement surgery and were now willingly giving of their time and expertise to help others at various stages of the recovery process. The attitude promoted was one of unquestionable advocacy for knee replacement surgery regardless of age or situation . . . I needed to look deeper. So, of course, follow the money.

On their website, I found this statement:

> *While Bone Smart does receive limited support from organizations including orthopedic manufacturers, the manufacturers are not otherwise affiliated with BoneSmart. org and cannot be held responsible for the content contained herein. This website's content is managed by Bone Smart.*

Fair enough, but who owned Bone Smart? Further investigation on the website revealed that Bone Smart was a part of the consumer outreach division of "The Foundation Advanced Research Medicine, Inc." or (FARM). Interestingly, when I googled that name, nothing at all came up. The construction of the name seemed odd, like words were missing, and indeed they were. The full name of FARM was "The Foundation for Advancement in Research in Medicine, Inc." How odd that Bone Smart would incorrectly spell the name of its parent organization on its own website.

This sent me off to investigate the FARM website, where I found that Bone Smart was created as an international consumer awareness campaign . . .

> to help patient-consumers learn about the exciting new advances in hip and knee implant materials in 2005. Using the powerful reach of video, radio, television, print, CD-ROM and the Internet, Bone Smart® is a one-stop information and **clinic and hospital referral network** for patient-consumers looking for a user-friendly, neutral environment, to explore their options and find the doctor and implant that's right for their needs. Clinics in the referral network have access to the program and marketing resources to use in their own outreach and patient education programs.

As it turns out, FARM is generously supported by orthopedic manufacturers, including Zimmer Biomet, Medtronic, Conformis, Smith & Nephew, and Don Joy Orthopedics—to name a few. FARM, in essence, is a shell organization that hides the fact that Bone Smart is bankrolled by industry sources who use it as a clinic and hospital referral network, among other things.

This arrangement allows them to donate money liberally to a nonprofit (tax-deductible, of course) and maintain the illusion that Bone Smart is a nonpartisan, objective source of information rather than an industry-sponsored forum cheerleading the promotion of knee replacement surgery.

FARM also "actively pursues revenue sharing relationships with companies and other organizations who share their goal of improving the lives of people with orthopedic disabilities." And who might that be? As it turns out, the CEO of FARM, Richard Warner, is also the CEO of Joint Replacement Centers of America, LLC, a for-profit venture that builds free-standing outpatient surgical centers across America. More knee replacement surgeries given to younger ambulatory patients equals more cash for him and his outpatient centers.

After I wrote a blog post about this, I was contacted by a representative of Bone Smart to take the post down over a disputed fact. I deleted the item in question, and it remains one of my top posts, to the dismay of Bone Smart representatives.

Another great example of the unseen influences of corporations and special interest groups on the information and images the public receives every day in the news and elsewhere is given by Sharyl Attkisson, an investigative journalist based in Washington D.C. Her latest book, *Stonewalled* (Harper-Collins) addresses just the type of subterfuge that we have been examining.

She also has a wonderful TED Talk published on February 6, 2015, about the marketing of a fictitious cholesterol-lowering drug Cholextra, and how easy it is to be misled by the "Truman Show-esque" alternate reality created around you by the corporations themselves.

Here is a small sample:

> *It turns out the Facebook and Twitter accounts you found that were so positive [About Cholextra], were actually written by paid professionals hired by the drug company to promote the drug. The Wikipedia page had been monitored by an agenda editor, also paid by the drug company. The drug company also arranged to optimize Google search engine results, so it was no accident that you stumbled across that positive non-profit that had all those positive comments.*

The non-profit was, of course, secretly founded and funded by the drug company. The drug company also financed that positive study and used its power of editorial control to omit any mention of cancer as a possible side-effect. Once more, each and every doctor who publicly touted Cholextra or called the cancer link a myth, or ridiculed critics as paranoid cranks and quacks, or served on the government advisory board that approved the drug, each of those doctors is actually a paid consultant for the drug company.

As for your own doctor, the drug company, in fact, like many continuing medical education classes, sponsored the medical lecture he attended that had all those positive evaluations. And when the news reported on that positive study, it didn't mention any of that.[111]

A healthy dose of skepticism is always required.

FOLLOW THE MONEY

"Cui bono" is a Latin term that asks the question: "Who benefits?" Keep this question in mind as the media attempts to define the narrative. Who are the major beneficiaries of the story and the course of action suggested by the narrative? Propaganda is not cheap and money fuels the illusions, so track the money like a bloodhound. Don't trust any organization, nonprofit or otherwise, until you know who is sponsoring them financially. All groups or individuals are beholden to their financial wellspring.

This can be a very difficult, time-consuming and complex task. But then again, it can be as simple as searching the "About" button on an organization's website and continuing

111. Sharyl Attkisson TED Talk, Published on Feb. 6, 2015.

to track the links to the funding sources. You are looking for links like "Donors," "Partners," "Grants" and even "History." Once you have an idea of who is funding the organization, you can take a look at the financial statement that every nonprofit is required to complete—the IRS 990.

GuideStar is an organization that offers some of the most complete and up-to-date nonprofit data available on the web. It has a free subscription where you can look up an organization, and the IRS-990 form is just one quick link away. However, their best tools are, unfortunately, behind a paywall.

Additionally, Littlesis.org—a play on the meme "Big Brother" offers a free crowdsourced database that tracks and maps relationships between powerful people, corporations, and organizations. Their research is generally used to support progressive movements, and there is always a risk of bias with crowdsourcing, but still useful, I think.

Track money in and money out of an organization. Exceptional examples of people dedicated to deep diving the finances between foundations, businesses, government organizations and NGOs are Charles Ortel at Charlesortel.com and Corey Digs at Coreysdigs.com. If you are not familiar with viewing events through the wide-angle lens of financial connections and interconnections, you are in for a treat. The money does not lie.

By the way, this is true of scientific research as well. Don't trust any science or research until you know who is funding the research and if the researchers have any financial ties that would create a conflict of interest. Scientists are required by law to disclose conflicts of interest, and funders of the study must be named in the final draft of a publication.

This list is by no means exhaustive, and I don't claim to be an expert, but I realize that with the technological tools available, we have substantial power to critically evaluate witness credibility based on following the financial flows. Watch what's done and where the money goes, not what's said.

Look for Connections

And finally, look for connections between witnesses, the main players and even the minor actors and their relationships with the agencies, organizations and foundations that comprise the narrative. You will find, in a most amazing way, the same or similar cast of characters emerge from the shadows over and over again. Remember, birds of a feather flock together, so if a new unknown player comes up, his known association with previously confirmed bad actors should raise a red flag. How many negative associations does he have?

Two places to start your investigation are Wikipedia and InfluenceWatch. Each entry is only as good as the citations used. I don't trust either of them fully, but they can accelerate your research for the basic history of any person or organization you are tracking. From there, you can follow up on the citations or look up other people/organizations associated or connected with your target of interest. LittleSis can also help in establishing connections.

Find Real Authorities to Trust

Where does one go for "true" information after coming to grips with the massive betrayal by the media elite? This is the predicament many truth seekers find themselves in. Depending on the Internet as the primary source of news can feel like taking a chance on a dive restaurant—who knows what can and should be trusted? This doesn't mean you should throw in the towel and decide that it's impossible to distinguish fact from fiction or information from disinformation.

In Appendix B, there is a list of high-quality freedom-oriented websites that I categorize as right- or left-leaning. These websites challenge the mainstream news narratives in different ways and are a great place to start exploring information from outside the sanctioned orthodoxy. If they aggregate stories from other sources, you will get to know the slant of the authors they choose to reprint as well as the quality of their writing and content.

However, the best source of information is a trusted human source who has delivered reliable information over time. With their name and reputation on the line, they are motivated to keep your trust or risk losing listeners/supporters. Their biography should be prominently displayed as evidence that they are a real person with a real history. You don't have to agree with everything they communicate, but they must at least demonstrate the ability to interpret current and historical narratives accurately and wisely.

There are many who have been in the liberty network for years, delivering sound advice for free, while others have a subscription model. You can fast-track your learning experience by listening to current information and reviewing past data as well. It's much like the advantages associated with being an apprentice.

And you shouldn't necessarily let the price of a subscription turn you off. Generally, for a small fee, you can be up to speed much faster than if you had to work to gain the same breadth of information yourself by sifting through large assortments of videos and sites that aggregate clickbait storylines and tease "miraculous" outcomes and fantastic scenarios.

Anonymous sources of information should never be considered as a primary resource. Don't waste your time picking through random videos, even if interesting and entertaining, from people you don't know from a hole in the ground. Test real individuals and move on from those who have failed. Eventually, you will have five to ten trusted sources that become your "go-to" sources as you attempt to interpret the ever-changing landscape of politics and media indoctrination.

WHISTLEBLOWERS

One particular type of individual who is almost always trust-worthy is the "whistleblower." He or she has paid a price in the past and generally remains in the line of fire in terms of a potentially tarnished reputation, social ostracism, public ridicule, and possible financial ruin in order to put alternative expert opinion into the public domain.

The whistleblower takes a big risk in pursuit of truth to warn of corruption within a specific domain of expertise. In short, they are motivated by the power of their convictions. They deserve careful attention lest we miss their message or warning.

As an insider within a large conglomerate, government agency, or profession, the whistleblower's opinion, should he choose to go rogue, will be censored because it challenges the prevailing opinion that has been elevated to a status that is beyond challenging. In a country that values freedom of speech, why should opposing viewpoints be censored?

As Weaver said prior to 1963, "But when there exists a practical monopoly of channels of information and communication, it is next to impossible to put another alternative before any sizable part of the population."[112]

The stories of whistleblowers are found in books, a few of which I discuss below, and on the Internet, but rarely within the mainstream media. The mainstream media generally refuses to publicize unorthodox opinions that could jeopardize their financial backing. In most cases, smear campaigns are launched against whistleblowers, and their lives are usually disrupted dramatically.

Anyone who has faced this type of opposition deserves the respect of a public hearing. The sacrifice and tenacity displayed in the face of overwhelming forces allied against them buttress their character and argue for the veracity of their claims.

112. Smith, 307.

THEIR STORIES

Here are some books about the lives of important whistleblowers in different fields whose stories might interest you.

MEDICINE

Dr. Marcia Angell

The Truth About the Drug Companies: How They Deceive Us and What to Do about It

> *During her two decades at* The New England Journal of Medicine, *Dr. Marcia Angell had a front-row seat on the appalling spectacle of the pharmaceutical industry. She watched drug companies stray from their original mission of discovering and manufacturing useful drugs and instead become vast marketing machines with unprecedented control over their own fortunes. She saw them gain nearly limitless influence over medical research, education, and how doctors do their jobs. She sympathized as the American public, particularly the elderly, struggled and increasingly failed to meet spiraling prescription drug prices. Now, in this bold, hard-hitting new book, Dr. Angell exposes the shocking truth of what the pharmaceutical industry has become—and argues for essential, long-overdue change.*

Andrew Wakefield

Callous Disregard: Autism and Vaccines – The Truth Behind a Tragedy

> *In 1995, Dr. Andrew Wakefield came to a fork in the road. As an academic gastroenterologist at the Royal Free School of Medicine and the University of London, he was confronted by a professional challenge and a moral choice. Previously*

healthy children were, according to their parents, regressing into autism and developing intestinal problems. Many parents blamed the MMR vaccine. Trusting his medical training, the parental narrative, and, above all, the instinct of mothers for their children's well-being, he chose what would become a very difficult road. Callous Disregard *is the account of how a doctor confronted first a disease and then the medical system that sought and still seeks to deny that disease, leaving millions of children to suffer and a world at risk.*

NATIONAL SECURITY APPARATUS

Edward Snowden

No Place to Hide: Edward Snowden, the NSA, and the U.S. Surveillance State by Glenn Greenwald

In May 2013, Glenn Greenwald set out for Hong Kong to meet an anonymous source who claimed to have astonishing evidence of pervasive government spying and insisted on communicating only through heavily encrypted channels. That source turned out to be the twenty-nine-year-old NSA contractor Edward Snowden, and his revelations about the agency's widespread, systemic overreach proved to be some of the most explosive and consequential news in recent history, triggering a fierce debate over national security and information privacy.

MEDIA

Sharyl Attkisson

The Smear: How Shady Political Operatives and Fake News Control What You See, What You Think, and How You Vote

Ever wonder how politics turned into a take-no-prisoners blood sport? The New York Times *bestselling author of* Stonewalled *pulls back the curtain on the shady world of opposition research and reveals the dirty tricks those in power use to influence your opinions. Behind most major political stories in the modern era, there is an agenda; an effort by opposition researchers, spin doctors, and outside interests to destroy an idea or a person. The tactic they use is the Smear. Every day, Americans are influenced by the Smear without knowing it. Paid forces cleverly shape virtually every image you cross. Maybe you read that Donald Trump is a racist misogynist, or saw someone on the news mocking the Bernie Sanders campaign. The trick of the Smear is that it is often based on some shred of truth, but these media-driven "hit pieces" are designed to obscure the truth. Success hinges on the Smear artist's ability to remain invisible; to make it seem as if their work is neither calculated nor scripted. It must appear to be precisely what it is not.*

EDUCATION

John Taylor Gatto

Dumbing Us Down: The Hidden Curriculum of Compulsory Schooling

After over 100 years of mandatory schooling in the U.S., literacy rates have dropped, families are fragmented, learning "disabilities" are skyrocketing, and children and youth are increasingly disaffected. Thirty years of teaching in the public school system led John Taylor Gatto to the sad conclusion that compulsory governmental schooling is to blame, accomplishing little but to teach young people to follow orders like cogs in an industrial machine. He became a fierce advocate of families and young people taking back education and learning, arguing that "genius is as common as dirt," but that conventional schooling is driving out the natural curiosity and problem-solving skills we're born with, replacing it with rule-following, fragmented time, and disillusionment.

Don't Be Afraid to Stand Face First into the Wind

As we have seen, manipulation of public opinion has been around since the 1900s, but the accelerated pace of "groupthink" and the growth of censorship in the 21st century is alarming. To think independently will require the courage to stand in the face of opposition. In the words of George Orwell, "In an age of universal deceit, telling the truth is a revolutionary act."

If you are taking flak from the media, then you are over the target. Don't expect a comfortable life as a truth seeker. You will need a stiff spine and a courageous heart, similar to the whistleblowing heroes that you've just read about.

Loving Truth

For most people today, "truth" is a foreign concept. The idea embodied by the word "truth" has been confused with "fact" and debased by relativity such that nothing is considered firm or fixed. The concept is in danger of being lost through drift and neglect, similar to the way that awareness of "propaganda" has been lost.

In a culture such as ours, an endorsement to love the truth sounds odd and out of place—almost Pollyannaish. But ancient thinkers believed that love of the right things and not just knowledge of them was the first principle of a proper education.

> *St. Augustine defines virtue as "Ordo Amoris," the ordinate condition of the affections in which every object is accorded that kind and degree of love which is appropriate to it. Aristotle says that the aim of education is to make the pupil like and dislike what he ought. When the age for reflective thought comes, the pupil who has been thus trained in "ordinate affections" or "just sentiments" will easily find the first principles in Ethics; but to the corrupt man they will never be visible at all and he can make no progress in that science. Plato before him had said the same. The little human animal will not at first have the right responses. It must be trained to feel pleasure, liking, disgust, and hatred at those things, which really are pleasant, likable, disgusting, and hateful.*[113]

As this passage implies, training your heart to love truth might not come naturally. Why would that be? If we consider the common idioms "facing the truth" or "the truth hurts," it gives us a glimpse of the difficulty of the task.

Jack Nicholson's character in the movie *A Few Good Men* famously declared, "You can't handle the truth." There is something about truth that is hard to receive. It resides outside our consciousness and beckons to us. It is simultaneously called the patterns of nature, the cosmic order, natural law, or The Way.

C. S Lewis explained truth in this way:

> *This conception [of truth] in all its forms, Platonic, Aristotelian, Stoic, Christian, and Oriental alike, I shall*

---

113. C.S Lewis, "The Abolition of Man." in *The Essential C.S. Lewis,* Dorsett, ed., (New York, 1988), 434.

henceforth refer to for brevity simply as "the Tao." Some of the accounts of it, which I have quoted, will seem, perhaps, to many of you merely quaint or even magical. But what is common to them all is something we cannot neglect. It is the doctrine of objective value, the belief that certain attitudes are really true, and others really false, to the kind of thing the universe is and the kind of things we are.[114]

It is correspondence with reality—the way things truly are in the cosmos. In our state of incomplete understanding, the truth is often unwanted because it puts us in a place of humility to an understanding more real and more important than our whimsical and ofttimes self-centered selves.

Loving the truth therefore is connected with embracing correction, walking humbly and being willing to be taught of things outside one's current understanding being mindful that we have but a partial knowledge of even ourselves. Friends who tell you the truth are one of the most valuable things in the world. There are things each of us prefers . . . not to see.

As we learned in Chapter 2 from Gustave Le Bon, whoever supplies the masses with illusions will become their master. Who doesn't want to be told "good news?"

Embracing truth means facing reality that is unflattering, unsettling, harsh and ofttimes tragic. Are you willing to do that?

I started the chapter with a different idiom, "the truth will come out in the end." For truth seekers or lovers of truth, this is a reminder that the truth of a matter will not necessarily be easy to discern; work is involved. Powerful forces who stand to lose may be using all the resources available to them to prevent the truth from emerging, as whistleblowers who have lost their lives attempting to shine a light into dark and hidden things can attest. Seeking the truth is not for the faint of heart.

114. C.S Lewis, 435.

And finally, the ever-present danger of distraction will be an enemy of those who pursue the truth. "It is entirely possible that the true and authentic reality is being drowned out by the countless superficial information bits noisily and breathlessly presented in propaganda fashion."[115] Remain focused and dogged in your pursuit of truth. Foster love of truth wherever it takes you.

Indeed, our friend Pieper, who was introduced in an earlier chapter, reminds us of why a failure of truth in a society is so dangerous:

> *Public discourse, the moment it becomes neutralized with regard to the strict standard of truth, stands by its nature ready to serve as an instrument in the hands of any ruler to pursue all kinds of power schemes. Public discourse itself, separated from the standard of truth creates on its part, the more it prevails, an atmosphere of epidemic proneness and vulnerability to the reign of the tyranny.*[116]

According to the Tao, training to love liberty and freedom should take precedence over the craving of safety and security, which are secondary values. As we already learned, propaganda is frequently masked as being something desirable, beneficial, and held out as the reasonable thing. If you are not grounded in truth, then you will be much more susceptible to the propagandist's offer to protect you from harm, the climate, guns, fake news, hateful speech, and rejection. The propagandist offers safety and security by sleight of hand. Liberty is the primary value.

Loving and valuing safety and security over freedom is trading feathers for worms.

The main thing is to have a soul that loves the truth and harbors it where he finds it. And another thing: truth requires constant repetition, because error is being preached about us all the time, and not only by isolated individuals but by the masses. In the newspapers and encyclopedias, in schools and universities, everywhere error rides high and basks in the consciousness of having the majority on its side.

—JOHANN WOLFGANG VON GOETHE

115. Pieper, 33.
116. Pieper, 30–31.

The Skylark, By G. H. Charnley

One day long ago, over the hot sands of a Middle Eastern country, a white skylark flew in joyous loops about the sky. As she swooped near the earth, she heard a merchant cry out, "Worms! Worms! Worms for feathers! Delicious worms!"

The skylark circled about the merchant, hungry at the mention of worms, but puzzled as to what the merchant meant. Little did the skylark know that the merchant was the devil. And seeing that the skylark was interested, the devil motioned her nearer. "Come here, my little friend. Come! See the lovely worms I have!"

Cautiously, the skylark landed and cocked her head at the merchant. "Come! Taste the juicy worms!" The skylark became aware that she was, indeed, quite hungry. And these worms looked bigger and tastier than any she had ever dug for herself out of the hardscrabble ground of the desert. The skylark hopped closer and put her beak up close to the worm. "Two worms for a feather, my friend. Two worms for one!"

The skylark was unable to resist. And she had, after all, so many feathers. So, with a swift motion, she pulled out a feather—just a small one—from beneath her wing and gave it to the merchant. "Take your pick, my little friend . . . any two, your heart's desire!" And so the skylark quickly snatched up two of the plumpest worms and swallowed her meal with delight. Never before had she tasted such wonderful worms. With a loud chirp, she leapt into the air and resumed her joyful flight.

Day after day the skylark returned. And always the merchant had wonderful worms to offer: black ones and blue ones, red ones and green ones, all fat and shiny and iridescent. But one day, after eating her fill, the skylark leapt again into the air and to her horror, she fell to the ground with a thud. She was unable to fly!

All at once, with a shock, she realized what had happened. From the delicious worms she had grown fatter and fatter; and as she plucked her feathers one by one, first her body, then her tail, and finally her very wings had grown balder and balder.

Horrified, she remembered how, slowly, imperceptibly, day by day, it had been getting harder and harder to fly; and how she had told herself it was no matter; she could always stop before it was too late. Now, suddenly, here she was, trapped on the ground. She looked up and saw the merchant looking at her. Was that a small, sly grin spreading across his face?

In terror, the skylark ran off into the desert. She ran and ran and ran and ran. It took her hours and hours. Never in her entire life had she walked nor run so far. Finally, she came to the softer ground near the desert springs where, before she met the merchant, she daily had come to dig for herself the small, dusty brown desert worms that could be found around the springs.

The skylark dug and dug in a frenzy. She piled up worm after worm until it was nearly dark. Then, wrapping her catch in a small fallen palm frond, she dragged it off back across the sand to where she saw the merchant, closing up his stall for the night.

The skin around her beak had grown bruised and tender; her small feet were bleeding from the great distances she had been forced to walk. "Oh, merchant! Oh, merchant! Please help me! Please help me! I cannot fly anymore! Oh, dear what shall I do? Please, please, take these worms from me and give me back my feathers!"

The merchant bent down and peered at the terrified skylark. He threw back his head and roared with laughter, a gold tooth, glinting in the red and setting sunlight. "Oh, I'll take those worms all right, my friend. A few weeks in this good soil and they, too, will be fat and green and glistening."

He unwrapped the worms and tossed them into a jar of black and humid soil. "But feathers?" He laughed again. "What will you do with feathers? Glue them on with spit?" He wheezed and cackled at his little joke. "Besides my friend," the merchant reached down and grabbed the already plucked and fattened skylark, "that's not my business—'feathers for worms.' Oh no . . ." He threw the skylark into a cage, . . . my business is WORMS FOR FEATHERS!'"

The merchant slammed the little cage door shut, smiled hungrily at his victim, and with a loud SNAP! of his fingers, he vanished into the desert air.[117]

This story is a reminder that life is difficult; scrapping for small dusty brown desert worms is hard work. Something too good to be true usually is . . . That is the illusion held out by the propagandist. If you incline your heart toward truth, then deceptive messages crafted to enslave and destroy will fail miserably. You will be able to stand on the courage of your convictions, on self-reliance, responsibility, and the love and commitment of community.

117. G. H. Charnley, *The Skylark*.

Chapter 12

ERA OF CROWDS OVER?

The main purpose of this book is to help you come to recognize the extent of the propaganda machine currently operating in this country as well as the resulting tyranny. This has been done through an examination of history and the writings of prominent leaders. Here are the main points of emphasis.

TEN MAJOR SUMMARY POINTS TO CONSIDER

1. WWI was the first large-scale demonstration of the manipulation of public opinion by utilizing every technique known at the time.

2. The ability to manufacture ideas or public opinion changed the entire power structure in the United States.

3. "Stagecraft" was the original fake news.

4. Faith in democracy was eclipsed by the growing consensus among leaders that technocrats and enlightened leaders

should now manufacture consent in the best interest of an unknowing public. The news became the collateral damage of this poisonous philosophy.

5. Manipulation of language for purposes other than the pursuit of truth is the first sign of tyranny.

6. Propaganda, having gone underground, is more dangerous than ever before, precisely because its machinations are now hidden.

7. Propaganda is a sophisticated set of techniques employed by the rich, impoverishing the marketplace of ideas and drowning out small voices.

8. Propaganda is hard to detect because much of the Infrastructure of Belief has been captured in order to influence people in ways that are not rational and that appeal to base desires that are cloaked in beneficial offerings such as safety and security.

9. Identification of propaganda includes a thorough understanding of the model and the ability to follow the money, appreciate whistleblowers, ask questions, dig deeper, and love the truth.

10. Leadership, words, and the quest for truth are the primary antidotes to the abuse of language and the tyranny that follows in its wake.

If the 19th century was renowned for the great Industrial Revolution, the 20th century should be renowned for the creation and refinement of the "Influence Revolution" or, as John Maxwell Hamilton, author of *Manipulating the Masses* calls it, the "Information State." A juggernaut was born—the power to control and regiment the masses according to the will of others without their knowledge.

The annals of history are silent and fail to record how the ideal conditions for propaganda enhancement were noiselessly harnessed and perfected via evolving technique, plentiful cash outlays, and extensive practice by a relative few who understood its potential.

And yet, where is any reference to this in the history books? How is it not common knowledge as a pivotal part of our history and heritage? **How is it possible that one of the greatest innovations of the twentieth century is largely unknown?**

Could it be that this was purposeful? Gutting the word "propaganda" of its menace to a fully functioning democracy was extremely advantageous to practitioners. The knowledge base that was needed to grow and expand the influence revolution was scattered throughout disparate areas of academia, including media, psychology, sociology, public relations, news, linguistics, and advertising. The seeds of propaganda transformed into a virtually unrecognizable multi-headed hydra.

The rise of mass media and the unprecedented success of WWI propaganda forever changed the balance of democratic power, tipping it toward the hand of a remote elite, the financially endowed who could command the techniques used to control the masses.

Elite thinkers, like Lippmann, abandoned the principles of democracy, declaring the masses utterly contemptible and unable to think adequately for themselves in a complex society. The subconscious fears and anxieties of the masses would, in the future, be manipulated to point them toward the "good of society" as determined by this same elite.

In the early 1900s, it was probable that someone with money was influencing citizens at a subconscious level. This was accomplished using hijacked authority, fake news events, and magnifying the influence of their messages through an enormous media "megaphone."

Currently, it is absolutely certain to be the case.

Propaganda will never die out. Intelligent men must realize that propaganda is the modern instrument by which they can fight for productive ends and help to bring order out of chaos.
—EDWARD BERNAYS

The end result of widespread propaganda use, as clearly stated by Pieper, can be nothing less than tyranny, whether you recognize it or not. But recognize it you must and be ready to act. Listen to Aleksandr Solzhenitsyn's warning and his lament that many had missed the opportunity to act decisively when Russian tyranny spread over the country.

> *And how we burned in the camps later, thinking: What would things have been like if every Security operative, when he went out at night to make an arrest, had been uncertain whether he would return alive and had to say goodbye to his family?*
>
> *Or if, during periods of mass arrests, as for example in Leningrad, when they arrested a quarter of the entire city, people had not simply sat there in their lairs, paling with terror at every bang of the downstairs door and at every step on the staircase, but had understood they had nothing left to lose and had boldly set up in the downstairs hall an ambush of half a dozen people with axes, hammers, pokers, or whatever else was at hand? . . .*
>
> *The Organs would very quickly have suffered a shortage of officers and transport and, notwithstanding all of Stalin's thirst, the cursed machine would have ground to a halt! If . . . if . . . We didn't love freedom enough. And even more—we had no awareness of the real situation. . . . We purely and simply deserved everything that happened afterward.*[118]

118. Solzhenitsyn, 13.

Losing Reality Bit by Bit

Every ten years, a generation that has been raised in comparative freedom from propaganda dies off and is replaced by a generation incubated and grown up in a culture of deception. How much longer before the ability to think for oneself is completely extinguished?

Will there be anyone alive who can lead us back to the "old" idea of truth and authentic relationships that existed prior to the propaganda tsunami that was unleashed in the 20th century and now pervades the 21st century?

What happens when even the desire for truth has been obliterated, and all that remains is fictitious reality masking the underlying tyranny that is willingly accepted by the stupefied masses?

Those who were alive during the middle of the great propaganda debate and perceived the danger were true prophets of the age.

Mighty little force is needed to control a man whose mind has been hoodwinked; contrariwise, no amount of force can control a free man, a man whose mind is free. No, not the rack, not fission bombs, not anything— you can't conquer a free man; the most you can do is kill him.
—Robert A. Heinlein

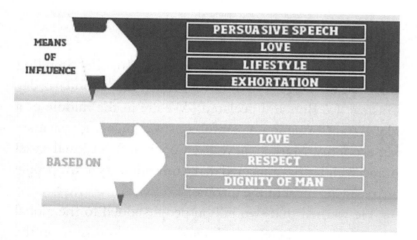

They had ominous words to say about the future of mankind, Aldous Huxley being the most prominent.

There will be, in the next generation or so, a pharmacological method of making people love their servitude, and

*producing dictatorship without tears, so to speak, pro-
ducing a kind of painless concentration camp for entire
societies, so that people will in fact have their liberties
taken away from them, but will rather enjoy it, because
they will be* **distracted from any desire to rebel by propaganda or brainwashing, or brainwashing enhanced by
pharmacological methods.** *And this seems to be the final
revolution.*[119]
—Aldous Huxley 1958 in *Brave New World Revisited*

*For the general public is being reduced to a state where peo-
ple not only are unable to find out about the truth but also
become unable even to search for the truth because they are
satisfied with deception and trickery that have determined
their convictions, satisfied with a fictitious reality created
by design through the abuse of language.*[120]
—Josef Pieper 1974 in *Abuse of Language, Abuse of Power*

GLOBAL PRESSURE COOKER

At a TED talk in Prague in February 2016, Guy Standing
stood on the stage sounding very much like a modern-day
Gustave Le Bon and declared, "We are in the middle of a
global transformation, a painful construction of a global market economy. Markets have been open and yet intellectual
property rights have ensured that a tiny minority of the people
are receiving most of the income."[121]

He warned that two billion people added to the global
labor market had created a huge downward pressure on the
wages in Europe, the United States and Japan and predicted
that they wouldn't rise in the foreseeable future. Arising from

---

119. Huxley, 253.
120. Pieper, 35.
121. https://www.youtube.com/watch?v=nnYhZCUYOxs.

that growing inequality and insecurity, he saw a new class structure emerging in the world.

At the top of the food chain: the oligarchy holding more and more of the world's wealth and power; the Salariat, people well employed with pensions and paid holidays followed by the old proletariat made up of the shrinking working class. And finally, just above the poor sits a growing class of millions he calls The Precariat.

The Precariat is composed of three different groups, Atavists, Migrants and Progressives whose lives are punctuated by instability and, in some cases, whose educational standing makes them overqualified for the work they are doing. They are offered no benefits and face a life of economic uncertainty teetering on the edge of a debt cliff. They are the first class in history losing the great rights, political, social, civil, and cultural.

Standing warns ominously, "This situation is not an accident but is desired by global capitalism, and it will not go away."[122]

The Atavists are defined as those who are angry at the great replacement of constitutional rights for a collective ideology. Looking backward to the good old days, they are vulnerable to the rhetoric of "neo-fascist populists" or "nationalists." The migrants are those whose lives have been disrupted through no fault of their own and who are angry living as outsiders in alien cultures. And finally, there are the progressives, educated but financially crippled by debt and disenfranchised with their prospects for the future.

Hence, the basic income distribution structure of the 20th century is broken and is not coming back. Too many people with too much insecurity will lose the capacity to be rational, and this will invariably lead to the "politics of inferno."

122. Ibid.

Can you hear shades of Gustave Le Bon? The sheep are waking to the realization that they are being robbed and pilfered by the wolves. An unsettled anger is growing just beneath the surface. As Le Bon wrote,

> *"like the sphinx of ancient fable: it is necessary to arrive at a solution to the problems offered by their psychology [the Crowd] or to resign ourselves to being devoured by them."*[123]

The sphinx of ancient fable sat on the edge of town, waiting to devour those who could not answer the riddle posed by the muse.

The riddle the wolves must answer? How to keep the sheep from waking up and recognizing that the rather odd-looking "sheep" on the perimeter of the field are actually wolves ready to devour them.

At the time of the industrial revolution, Le Bon's solution to the riddle posed by the angry mob was propaganda. Surround the sheep with layer upon layer of deception and tell them the illusions they want to hear. Keep them fat and happy while we erect the holding pens . . . oops, I mean global framework of governance.

A century later, the elite remain haunted and threatened but this time by a new wave of anger signaling a partial awakening of the sheep to the bitter realities of the political, social, economic and ideological architecture of control erected around them.

What will quell the masses this time?

According to Standing, the only way to avoid this "politics of inferno" is to build a new income distribution system suited to the 21st century—the universal basic income.

Allow me to paraphrase, you my little sheep should gladly accept a meager subsistence and the exchange of the great rights—for simple security.

123. Le Bon, 61.

Standing's favorite slogan: "basic security as equality." Or . . . worms for feathers.

Not surprisingly, professor Standing is a founding member and the current co-president of BIEN or Basic Income Earth Network, launched in 1986, which has been religiously marketing the Universal Basic Income concept to the world. His latest book, *The Precariat: The New Dangerous Class* (2021), has already been translated into sixteen languages.

Leadership – The Antidote to Propaganda

In 1896, Le Bon confidently took up his pen and announced to the world, "The age we are to enter will in truth be the ERA OF CROWDS."

In the era of crowds, individuals do not exist; their hopes are inconsequential, their dreams irrelevant, and their freedoms tethered to the good of the collective. The only thing that matters is the group and what the planners have in mind. All that matters is the faceless crowd marching to the tune being played for them.

Control ideas, and you control the planet. Ideas are the most powerful force on the planet. Bombs and machine guns are no match for the power of an idea whose time has come.

Creative and life-giving ideas will be rejected and pulverized with Operation Spider's Web as well as the people who hold them. The Media Industrial Complex sits as the howitzer on the hill. Try to buck the narrative, and you will be firewalled.

When you want to help people, you tell them the truth. When you want to help yourself, you tell them what they want to hear.
—Thomas Sowell

The media complex is the vital nerve center critical to the capture and manipulation of each pillar in The Infrastructure of Belief. Imagination is crushed and trivialized by a thousand banal and thoughtless influences through Hollywood. The marketplace of ideas is crippled by the media that defines the terms of debate, the limits of discussion, and the screening of the talking heads. Experiences are manipulated and problems magnified through stagecraft and well-written marketing plans. Authorities are handpicked and framed to protect the all-glorious narrative of orthodoxy and the weight of social pressure leveraged against the heretics among us.

Without its destruction, we are deceiving ourselves that any changes can be long-lasting. The cartel must be broken for liberty to flourish.

What good is the First Amendment, the right to free speech, when this leviathan exists—this perverse accessory to the crimes of tyranny and greed?

And what of us—the crowd? Could the propagandists have achieved their vision without the assistance of individuals who might have been leaders in the past but who have been bought off and co-opted by large moneyed interests?

They are the epitome of Nietzsche's last man who cares for nothing but comfort.

Citizens of the world are waiting for bold leaders to arise from every country and in every institution to throw off the overloads and end the era of crowds.

. . . Say MY name.

Those bold ones, of all creatures on the face of the earth, are to be feared by that class of men who now rule from a distance with numbers, verbiage, trickery, and bribes.

. . . Say OUR names, one by one. We are NOT a crowd.

Cracks are beginning to show in the Land of Oz. Not all the leaders have been demoralized and weakened. Belief that the news can be trusted is at an all-time low. Belief that politicians, left or right, are doing the people's bidding is at an all-time low. The curtain of deception hiding the "Great Oz" is slowly being drawn back to reveal the "little Oz" with a giant megaphone.

The propagandist isn't so powerful after all . . . once we see behind the curtain!

I have sworn upon the altar of God Eternal, hostility against every form of tyranny over the mind of man.

—THOMAS JEFFERSON

EPILOGUE

Sons of Gondor! Of Rohan! My brothers! I see in your eyes the same fear that would take the heart of me! A day may come when the courage of men fails, when we forsake our friends and break all bonds of fellowship. But it is not this day. An hour of wolves and shattered shields when the age of Men comes crashing down! But it is not this day! This day we fight! By all that you hold dear on this good Earth, I bid you stand! Men of the West!

—*Aragorn, the* Lord of the Rings *at the last battle*

Game on Oligarchs

Your Time Is Short

Men of the West, Arise!

APPENDIX A

Forms of Idea Censorship

Here is a list of different ways ideas competing with the dominant narrative can be controlled and/or suppressed.

Simple Suppression

Regulating down the amount of time competing views and their promoters are allowed in the media. This includes shadow banning—the outright banning of unacceptable content.

Distortion

Distortion of alternative views includes the partial or incomplete renderings of competing views to prevent a true picture of the idea.

Discrediting without Refuting

Taking some doctrine or opinion and treating it as if it were a universally accredited dogma, By this means of misrepresentation the propagandist assumes either boldly or blandly that everyone in his right mind accepts the opinion as a necessary presupposition, and then he proceeds to build his case upon it. The effect of this maneuver is to keep the proposition, which is essential to the argument away from public criticism.

Discrediting with Supposed Refuting

The Commission: Another clever trick of politicians is the use of a commission to discredit alternative narratives. The panel members are selected from a reliable network of hacks who can be counted on to render a predetermined outcome regardless of the facts. This commission can narrow witness lists, control questioning, "interpret the data" insufficiently, and then declare the "truth" to the public, generally years later, after many of the initial facts have been forgotten.

Fact-checkers: A relatively new phenomenon is the rise of fact-checker organizations ostensibly created to control the spread of "fake news." In reality, they exist to discredit sources of information outside the narratives of Operation Spider's Web.

Reframing Competing Ideas as Hurtful and Offensive

Ideas reframed as hurtful or offensive require social control for the benefit of the vulnerable population being "harmed." This can result in criminalization of those views and is an overt sign of totalitarianism.

Allow for Left and Right Political Dissent

The importance of this strategy is to ensure that the playing field of ideas still looks level even though it no longer is. It simulates the illusion of free speech, an extremely important deception in a supposedly democratic society.

Forms of People Censorship

In forming Operation Spider's Web, it's important not only to censor ideas but also to discredit the people that hold them.

Mockery and Ridicule without Refuting

One of the first lines of defense against people who will not refrain from disseminating ideas that threaten the pseudo-reality being created is general mocking and ridicule. People do not like to be made light of or held in low esteem, especially in front of a national audience. Use of the terms "conspiracy theory" or "conspiracy theorist" is another powerful way to discredit without refuting.

De-platforming on Social Media Outlets

Those who persist in their outrageous behavior of questioning the narrative can simply be de-platformed from social media. This can have harsh ramifications by throttling income from those same platforms and significantly reducing their ability to spread "dangerous" messages.

APPENDIX B

FREEDOM-ORIENTED SITES – RIGHT LEANING

Breitbart News

The Daily Caller

The Epoch Times

The Gateway Pundit

Conservative Treehouse

World Net Daily

Children's Health Defense
  Network

Red State

Peter Breggin: Breggin.com

Joel Skousen: World Affairs
  Brief

Catherine Austin Fitts:
  The Solari Report

Dr. Joseph P. Farrell
  Gizadeathstar.com

FREEDOM-ORIENTED SITES – LEFT LEANING

Paul Craig Roberts

Global Research

Zero Hedge

Off-Guardian.org

C.J. Hopkins Substack

Dr. Naomi Wolf Substack

Jon Rappoport Substack or
  Nomorefakenews. com

The Intercept

Steve Kirsch Substack

Mark Crispin Miller
  Substack

John Whitehead
  The Rutherford Institute

Dan Sheehan
  danielpsheehan.com

RECOMMENDED READING

PR! A Social History of Spin, by Stuart Ewen
1984, by George Orwell
Brave New World, by Aldous Huxley
Brave New World Revisited, by Aldous Huxley
Abuse of Language, Abuse of Power, by Josef Pieper
Propaganda, by Edwards Bernays
Crystallizing Public Opinion, by Edwards Bernays
The Crowd: A Study of the Popular Mind, by Gustave Le Bon
How We Advertised America, by George Creel
Propaganda: The Formation of Men's Attitudes,
   by Jacques Ellul
Public Opinion, by Walter Lippmann
The Phantom Public, by Walter Lippmann
In Defense of Tradition, by Richard Weaver
Manufacturing of Consent, by Noam Chomsky
Walter Lippmann and the America Century, by Ronald Steel
Propaganda Technique in the World War, By Harold Lasswell
*Propaganda and Promotional Activities: An Annotated
   Bibliography,* by Harold Lasswell et al.
The Open Conspiracy: What Are We To Do With Our Lives?
   by H.G. Wells

ABOUT THE AUTHOR

A lifelong reader and explorer of truth, Ms. Stiles was stunned to personally experience the malevolent evil that had overtaken the leadership of an inner city school district in which she had volunteered. Being honored as "Citizen of the Year" did nothing to dispel the shocking realization of the broad and sweeping corruption. This experience propelled her to a deep historical search into the roots of public education and beyond. A teacher by nature and a contrarian by design, she has a keen ability to simplify the complex and make seminal older works accessible to the modern mind in a fresh and easy rendering.

She has previously authored two works: *Fast Track Your Recovery from a Total Knee Replacement: How to Eliminate Pain and Pain Medicine the Quickest Way Possible* and *Color and Laugh Your Way to Knee Replacement Recovery*. She is also the inventor of the Flex Bar, a recovery tool for knee replacement surgery.

Told by a university professor that there was no such thing as a renaissance woman and that she should cap her B.S. in Physical Therapy and M.S. in Exercises Science with a Ph.D. in the sciences, she promptly completed an M.A. in Practical Theology.

While the writing of *One Idea to Rule Them All* by a physical therapist may seem like a metaphysical oddity or quirk of the universe, it is simply the product of an active mind in the quest for truth. The barriers to accurate perception today are plentiful and well laid out in this book, which serves as a concise guide to unveiling the machinations of idea bullying so that they are easily recognizable by those of high school age and beyond; to those of both right and left persuasion—in short, to anyone who senses in their bones that something in the world is off-kilter and can't quite put their finger on the source.

19430934R00146